FOR
JOHN YOUELL, *ESQ.*
HE LOVED BOOKS AND KNOWLEDGE
AND THE PACIFIC OCEAN

Alejandro Malaspina
(Museo Naval Coll.)

VOYAGES
OF
ENLIGHTENMENT

Thomas Vaughan

E. A. P. Crownhart-Vaughan

Mercedes Palau de Iglesias

Malaspina on the Northwest Coast
1791 / 1792

NORTH PÁCIFIC STUDIES

Explorations of Kamchatka: North Pacific Scimitar. by Stepan P. Krasheninnikov. Translated and edited by E. A. P. Crownhart-Vaughan. OHS, 1972.

Colonial Russian America: Kyrill T. Khlebnikov's Reports, 1817-1832. Translated and edited by Basil Dmytryshyn and E. A. P. Crownhart-Vaughan. OHS, 1976.

Printed in USA
Glass-Dahlstrom Printers
Portland, Oregon

Acknowledgments

This work was made possible through the cooperation and support of many persons and the institutions with which they are associated. Their generous assistance is deeply appreciated.

The National Endowment for the Arts, through a grant to the Museum of New Mexico, made the original part of this exhibition possible. Through a further generous grant to the Oregon Historical Society we have been able to enrich the exhibition and emphasize certain larger aspects of the Malaspina Expedition as it pertains to our own sphere of interest, the North Pacific Ocean.

Our most profound thanks to the New Mexico instigators of the exhibition for their original initiative: Richard Polese, Director, and Michael Weber, Associate Director, the Museum of New Mexico; and Donald C. Cutter, Professor of History, the University of New Mexico.

Our colleagues in Spain who have given so willingly of their personal time, their knowledge and their collections for our Oregon exhibition include:

Madrid: *Museo de America:* Don Carlos Martinez Barbeito, Director; and Antonio de Inglesias, volunteer. *Museo Naval:* Captain Don Roberto Barreiro-Meiro, Director; and Dona Maria Cruz Alonso Ruiz. *Instituto Historico de Marina:* Captain Don Jose Maria Zumalacarregui Calvo, Director. *Direccion General de Relaciones Culturales, Ministerio de Asuntos Exteriores:* Don Marcelino Oreja Ajuirre, Minister: Don Alfonso de la Serna; and Don Julio Sousa, who was especially helpful. At the *Biblioteca Nacional* our special thanks to Don Hipolito Escolar, Director; Don Roberto Liter, Secretary; and Dona Elena Santiago, Mapas y Planas. *Jardin Botanico de Madrid:* Don Salvador Riva Martinez, Director; and Don Aurelio Sobrino, Librarian. *Archivo Historico Nacional:* Don Luis Sanchez-Belda, Director. *Real Academia de la Historia;* Don Dalmiro de la Valgoma y Diaz-Varela.

Barcelona: *Museo Maritimo:* Don Jose Maria Martinez-Hidalgo y Teran, Director; and Captain Don Laureano Carbonell Relat, Conservator. *Museo Etnologico:* Don Augusto Panyella y Gomez, Director; and Dona Carmen Huera Cabeza. *Archivo de la Corona de Aragon:* Don Federico Udina Martorell, Director; and Dona Maria Mercedes Costa Paretas. *Real Academia de Ciencias y Artes:* Don L. Lole Sabaris. *Universidad de Barcelona:* Don Vernet, Professor of the History of Science.

Seville: *Archivo General de Indias:* Dona Rosario Parras Cala, Director. *Univer-*

sidad de Sevilla: Don Francisco Morales Padron.

Cadiz: Real Academia Hispano-Americana: Don Jose Paria Peman y Pemartin.

Jerez de la Frontera: Archivo Municipal; Don Manuel Antonio Garcia Paz, Director. Don Ramon Guerrero of this city has been most gracious.

Simancas: Archivo General de Simancas: Don Amando Represa, Director; and Dona Maria Carmen Fernandez.

We wish to thank most particularly the great friends and patrons of the Oregon Historical Society, Edmund Hayes, the late John Youell, former Chairman of the North Pacific (Irkutsk) Archival Research Group, and Mrs. Jane West Youell; Samuel S. Johnson, present Chairman of that Group, and Mrs. Elizabeth Johnson; the Northwest Area Foundation, Westland Foundation, and S. S. Johnson Foundation; and Dr. John Steelquist.

At the Oregon Historical Society Robert Stark, Museums Administrator, has been responsible for coordinating all aspects of the exhibition as it is presented in Oregon. Chief Photographer Maurice Hodge has made the meticulous photocopies of materials too fragile to leave Spain. Priscilla Knuth, Editor, and Bruce Hamilton, Associate Editor, have faithfully encouraged and assisted the authors. Mr. Hamilton's design of this book is especially appreciated. We also recognize the assistance of Cameron C. R. Vaughan.

To all we express our most heartfelt thanks for the aid which has made this important example of international scholarly cooperation possible.

Thomas Vaughan, Portland
E. A. P. Crownhart-Vaughan, Portland
Mercedes Palau de Iglesias, Madrid
August, 1977

Prologue

On the morning of 11 March 1778 Captain James Cook R.N. of H.M. Sloop of War *Resolution* tacked off the coast of "New Albion." In consort leading ahead was H.M.S. *Discovery*, Captain Charles Clerke R.N., who would succeed Cook after Kealakekua Bay and meet his death off Petropavlovsk, Kamchatka in late August, 1779.

Far up their port side was Cape Foulweather eleven leagues distant with Yaquina Head seven leagues away. Dead ahead lay Cape Perpetua. The consummate sailor wrote in his log:

Each extreme of the land that was now before us, seemed to shoot out into a point. The Northern one was the same which we had first seen on the 7th; and on that account, I called it *Cape Perpetua*. It lies in the latitude of 44°6' North, and in the longitude of 235°52' East. The Southern extreme before us, I named *Cape Gregory*. Its latitude is 43°30', and its longitude 235°57' East. It is a remarkable point; the land of it rising almost directly from the sea, to a tolerable height, while that on each side of it is low.

I continued standing off till one in the afternoon. Then I tacked and stood in, hoping to have the wind off from the land in the night. But in this I was mistaken.

And so Cook entered the scene of Spanish domination right on target at the site where Francis Drake 199 years earlier had sailed into the North American coastline to anchor for five days beneath the southern head of Cape Arago [Cape Gregory], a historic landfall predating the Jamestown and Plymouth Rock landings. Even more urgent, it was a landfall which laid claim to the New Albion coast by right of discovery, and would vex the Spaniards through succeeding generations as the mysterious and ill-defined coast came gradually to be known as the Oregon Country.

So here was Cook adding great laurels to his third voyage, but, by acts of God and unpredictable Pacific weather, missing the Columbia River mouth and the Strait of Juan de Fuca. He sailed on to death and glory, followed in 1785 by the magnificent French sailor le Comte de La Perouse in the *Boussole* and his lieutenant Paul-Antoine Vicomte Fleuriot de Langle in command of the *Astrolabe*. The French expedition followed Cook's northern route, reaching Mount St. Elias on June 23, 1786. La Perouse and his expedition met complete disaster in the Pacific in 1788. His Northwest Coast dispatches however had earlier been sent overland from Petropavlovsk across Siberia to Paris. His report on Russian movements down the Alaskan coast soon reached the ears of the Spanish court and St. Petersburg as well.

Russian hunters referred to the great land Bering discovered as "bolshaia zemlia," but to the Spanish there was room for only one majesty in that northern vastness. Their own. Theirs by right of Pacific Ocean discovery and all the daring voyages in subsequent centuries.

During this time of great international tension Alejandro Malaspina, an Italian captain in the Spanish Fleet, proposed an elaborate voyage of geographical and scientific discovery, one to rival Spain's imperial competitors—the British and the French. The voyage would accomplish more and be better publicized by its successful commander—Malaspina, himself.

VOYAGES
OF
ENLIGHTENMENT

Spanish Admiral Alejandro Malaspina exemplified the special flowering of the late 18th century Enlightenment, as did several officers of his expedition who shared his energetic scientific inquiries. Happily the robust Italian was closely studied at his state trial, and the description given is in harmony with his portrait in the commemorative exhibition. He was "of a grave and haughty aspect, with prominent features, a high serene forehead, a firm mouth and rather full lips, eyes not over large but expressive; and to complete the attractions of the. . .class which at first raised him high and later brought him down, his nose was generous and flaring, one of those which were in favor at the court of Maria Louisa." This somewhat oblique description suggests a romantic as well as a scientific disposition in the brilliant naval commander, born in Malazzo in the Duchy of Parma in 1754. Here in this Spanish possession his father, the Marques Carlos Morello, prepared him for a naval career. The reasons for so long a preparation are not presently known, but contrary to British practice Malaspina was no longer a boy when he arrived at the Departamento de Cadiz in November, 1774 as a midshipman. He completed the training requirements in two years, was promoted to second lieutenant and invested as Cabel-lero de Justicia in the Order of San Juan. January 1, 1776, he was assigned to a frigate on the Mediterranean Station, making occasional forays past Gibraltar into the Atlantic.

As a full lieutenant he served on the frigate *San Julian* attached to the squadron of Admiral Juan de Langara. This flotilla, consisting of eleven large ships and two frigates, encountered the English Admiral Sir George Rodney off Cape San Vincente on his way to a besieged Gibraltar. The Marques de Medina fought the *San Julian* valorously, but Rodney's 21 ships and ten frigates overpowered the Spanish force, accounting for seven vessels. The *San Julian* eventually escaped her British prize crew, but Malaspina had already been transferred to Gibraltar. Upon being exchanged he immediately returned to sea duty in February, 1780. Later Malaspina transferred to Algeciras where he participated in the memorable but unsuccessful Siege of Gibraltar which was held by English forces under General Sir George Elliot.

Malaspina escaped unscathed in the bloody melees of the famous fortified floating batteries of engineer J.C.E. d'Arcon immediately under Gibraltar's walls. He fought again under General Luis de Cordova against another stout admiral, Earl Howe, in the action at Cape Espartel where Howe and his convoy outsailed and outfought a larger fleet resisting the relief of Gibraltar. On December 29 of the same year (1782) Malaspina was promoted Captain of a frigate. In command of the *Asuncion* he voyaged to the Philippines and to India, returning to Cadiz in 1784. After some months of training duty ashore, he began a voyage around the world in the frigate *Astrea*.

The young commander visited many ports along the east coast of South America, rounded Cape Horn to Callao, the port of Lima, and then pushed west to the Philippines. He returned from Manila to Cadiz via the Cape of Good Hope. It is said that during this long voyage Malaspina planned the details of a Spanish expedition which would follow the example of Captain James Cook and the French navigator le Comte de La Perouse, if not transcend their accomplishment. Although a true circumnavigation never occurred, his project was called the "Plan of a Scientific and Political Voyage Around the World." The Spaniard Martin Fernandes de Navarette later described it as "a most brilliant testimony; at the end of the past century it gave our government a laudable interest which served to augment the scientific knowledge of our globe." This was achieved by a country in political disarray and by a superb sailor-scientist who has unfortunately been lost from general view. One perceives that the end prospect or last act for great voyages of the Age of Enlightenment was unattractive. Cook was killed at the very least. Charles Clerke died of tuberculosis, La Perouse and his two ships' crews met death in the reefs of the New Hebrides, both

Malaspina and his contemporary George Vancouver ended up in unfair sequestration if not disgrace, not to mention William Broughton who was certainly reviled by his peers until his death in Florence. James King had died early on the French Riviera and John Gore sat as a post captain at Greenwich Hospital. Only the good humored Louis de Bougainville lived to old age and great honors.

Spanish Naval Minister Antonio Valdes began with the thought of remodeling the mortar ship *Santa Rosa* for the bold expedition, but Malaspina wanted two new ships, and he eventually undertook the construction of the 306-ton corvettes *Descubierta* (Discovery) and *Atrevida* (Daring)— 109 feet in length with a 14-foot draft loaded—best identified as sloops. He followed the early example of James Cook in this and other important details, mindful of the fact that a consort, large or small, could be of critical assistance in unknown waters and treacherous circumstances. One interesting detail is that Malaspina sheathed the hulls inside as well as out for further protection against rocks and shoals. He also solicited much professional advice from the new scientists and physicians concerning chronometers, other measuring instruments, related technical gear, as well as dietary suggestions.

The Spanish fleet physician Jose Salvaresa was very helpful with new findings in food and diet, a distinct advance over the previous generation when crews three times the size necssary for ship handling were routinely signed on to insure enough living hands to work the ship home. Malaspina checked on venting for air circulation and proper food storage and preparation. Certainly he was ahead of his time in experiments to distill water, prepare antiscorbutics, preserve meat and serve fresh fruits and vegetables. He ruled out almost all hard liquor and salted codfish and went into detail on proper clothing for the several climates the ships would enter. In writing his specific instructions to officers of the expedition Malaspina referred to his own sailing experiences as well as the feats of Cook and the French explorers.

He kept close watch on the yard officers and the arsenal, seeking always the best, and an adequate number. The ships carried six anchors between them and an adequate amount of cannon and shot, balancing this armament with a harpsichord. To Jose Bustamante, his second in command and captain of the *Atrevida*, he gave most tactful instruction: "In ordinary ships of the fleet discipline is imperative," but on this long voyage of discovery he wished to win obedience and discipline through example, "not what the orders are, but rather what can be done and with what intent. On this commission, the scientific aspect rather than the military is what will contribute to public usefulness." And so this well-favored leader strove in his best judgment toward the attainment of harmonious solutions for his men, "the essential basis of service." But to be realistic, these were much more than hydrographic surveys and collectors' dream voyages.

Astronomy and natural history were all very well, but the expedition was also instructed to assess the political and military situation in restive Spanish territories scattered across the globe. Most particularly an assessment was wanted in light of the important dispatches from St. Petersburg which the Marques de Almodovar, the Visconde de la Herreria and the Conde de Lacy, Minister of King Carlos III to the Court of Russia, through the years had sent to Secretary of State Marques de Grimaldi and Conde Floridablanca in Madrid. These cipher dispatches concerned Russian plans and encroachments along the Northwest Coast of America, long a Spanish sphere of interest. And now there were the grasping English, not to mention French designs.

Malaspina was formally promoted to Captain in the navy September 21, 1789, after he had held sea trials off the harbor of Cadiz and the expedition had sailed on its diagonal course down the Atlantic July 30. The corvettes passed the Canary Islands and the Cape Verdes, noted distant Trinidade in the log, and anchored off Montevideo, then an Argentine colony. They undertook a survey of the Rio de la Plata and the Patagonian coast down to Puerto Deseado, Argentina. They then separated to rendezvous at the Islas Malvinas (Falkland Islands), explored the forbidding east coast of Tierra del Fuego, and rounded the Horn far south at 62°.

Subsequently they touched at San Carlos de Chile, sailed north to Valparaiso, tacked outward to the islands of Juan Fernandez, the supposed site of Robinson Crusoe's shipwreck, and returned shoreward to visit Concepcion. Coquimbo, Chile, was followed by Callao, with a formal visit to Lima, capital of the viceroyalty of Peru. "Following the coast," they investigated Guayaquil on the Guayas River in Ecuador and moved up around the shoulder of

Tierra Firma and Costa Rica toward Panama. Noting the volcanoes of Guatemala on February 19, 1790, *Descubierta* pushed on through foul weather and headwinds toward New Spain. Bustamante, who was detached in Panama, had gone directly to Acapulco, arriving February 1. At that station he sent messages to the very able and newly arrived viceroy, the Conde de Revillagigedo in Mexico City, reporting the Expedition's progress and his intention to move on to San Blas ship repair yards after drawing a plan of Acapulco port. On March 26 he sailed north, and the following day Malaspina arrived in the same roadstead after "an exhausting journey."

March 29 Bustamante in *Atrevida* in the early afternoon "descried the coast of San Blas and especially the mountain of San Juan over the prow; its elevation and configuration at the summit served as a very certain landmark to find the port." There he was met by the famous Pacific navigator of 1775, Francisco de la Bodega y Quadra who had returned from Madrid with the newly appointed viceroy. As Commandante and Chief of the Departamento de San Blas, Bodega y Quadra offered all assistance to Bustamante's worn ship. The reenergized but ill-located depot of San Blas had been established in 1767 to give support and supplies to the northern presidios of Monterey, San Diego and Loreto, and to oppose Russian plans. As was proper, Bustamante accurately described the port of San Blas: "The town is located a quarter of a league from the arsenal. . .the village, reduced to a very few common structures, is comprised of huts covered with straw, presenting the picture of a poor miserable settlement located in an insane climate, inhabited only through necessity or because of the advantages which its preservation produces for the interest of the State. Several individual dwellings and a royal [official] structure are built with some solidarity."

As Bustamante supervised the repairs, a royal messenger arrived with jarring news. This was of course a time of great tension with the continuing reverberations from the Nootka imbroglio. Rather than continue on to the Sandwich Islands, to which Spain contested ownership by a centuries-old discovery claim on the Hawaiian archipelago, Madrid ordered Malaspina north. He was to determine the truth of the Maldonado memoir which had just been discovered in the Archivos del Duque de Infandato. The memoir stated that in 1588 Lorenzo Ferrer Maldonado had passed from the New England coast across to the Pacific near the 50th parallel. Of course, this impossible claim aside, the Spanish government was deeply interested in the new claims and contentions of the British through Cook (and no doubt intelligence of Vancouver's proposed voyage), the findings of La Perouse and the ever expanding claims of the Russian hunters (or *promyshlenniki*) hunting sea otter from the northwest south toward the Columbia River. A new plan was therefore drawn for Malaspina's perusal, to move far out from the coast to catch the northering wind, sail up to the 60th parallel, turn in to the unknown coast and sail south toward the 18,008 foot peak, Mount St. Elias. The passage described in the memoir would be located near that political marker; then if it were not found, the flotilla should continue south, tracing that part of the embayed coastline as yet unpenetrated by Spanish or other foreigners. After a stop at Nootka the commanders would sail toward the Oregon coast, to Monterey and on to Acapulco. On April 11 Bustamante received news of Malaspina's arrival in Acapulco, and on the 13th, sailed to join his chief for the northern passage. While the ships had made splendid progress around South America in a magnificent weathering cruise, the shakedown revealed some changes and adjustments to be necessary among the officers and crews for whom some brief biographical information follows.

Jose Bustamante y Guerra was born in Santander in 1757. He entered the navy at 11 years and rose to frigate command in 1784. In 1788 he assisted Malaspina in planning the Expedition. He successfully commanded the *Atrevida* until the final return to Spain. In 1795 he was made Governor of Uruguay and Naval Chief of the Viceroyalty of la Plata. In 1809 he became President of the Audiencia de Charcas y del Cuzco, of Peru. He then served as Captain General of Guatemala, and died in Madrid in 1825. His diary of the great voyage, *Viaje Politico-Cientifica Alrededor del Mundo* was published at last by Novo y Colson in Madrid in 1885.

Cayetano Valdes, subaltern to Malaspina, was a brother of Naval Minister Antonio Valdes. He sailed with Malaspina from Cadiz to Mexico and to the Northwest Coast. Upon returning to Mexico Malaspina and Mexican Viceroy Revillagigedo ordered him to prepare a second expedition to the Northwest Coast with *Dionisio Alcala-Galliano*, to explore the Strait of Juan de Fuca. Valdes returned to Spain via Mexico and participated in the historic battles off El Ferrol, La Coruna and Trafalgar (1805), commanding the ships *Pelayo* and *Neptune*, respectively. Although he served as Governor of strategic Cadiz he was twice exiled. In 1823 he was made Regente Provisional del Reino and then rose to the historic title Captain General of the Armada, or commander of the Spanish Fleet.

Two *Descubierta* subalterns, *Juan Bernacci* and *Secundino Salamanca*, returned north with Valdes and Alcala-Galliano in the schooners *Sutil* and *Mexicana*. They engaged in the successful explorations including Nootka and beyond the Strait of Juan de Fuca through what is now called the Inside Passage. *Rafael Rodriguez Arias* was a bookkeeper and *Jose de Mesa* served as chaplain. The surgeon and assistant to the botanist was *Francisco Flores*; *Fabioli Ponzani* served as midshipman.

Of greater interest to us is *Felipe Bauza y Canas*, in charge of drawing. He oversaw the preparation of all charts and maps of the Expedition. A native of Mallorca and a pilot's mate in the Spanish Fleet, Bauza had served a hard apprenticeship under Vicente Tofino preparing the *Atlas Maritimo* of Spain. In 1787 he was made Professor of Fortifications and Military Drawing in the Naval School of Cadiz where two years later he was promoted to lieutenant, obviously on merit. Malaspina had wanted him for the Expedition, and he worked intently drawing mostly coastal profiles from the Rio de la Plata all the way up to Alaska and among the islands of Oceania. When Bauza returned to the Americas in

July, 1793, he disembarked at Callao with Espinosa y Tello and sailed to Valparaiso in the frigate *El Aquila.* They traveled overland to Santiago, crossed the cordillera and the pampas to Buenos Aires and sailed thence to Spain.

When the Direccion Hidrografia was created in 1797 Bauza was named deputy chief, and there he initiated the publication of materials from the Expedition. This would have had special ramifications, with the leader then in disgrace. In 1807 Bauza became a member of the Royal Academy of History, presenting a paper on South American geography. When the Napoleonic armies invaded Spain Bauza placed the hydrographic archives in "twelve well loaded carts" and left Madrid for Cadiz. In 1815 he was named Director of the Direccion Hidrografia succeeding Espinosa y Tello. Bauza then worked on the *Atlas of North America* (1828) and the *Atlas of South America (1830).*

With the advent of the absolutist government of Ferdnando VII the liberal cartographer removed to London until his death in 1834, continuing studies in geography and cartography which brought him worldwide fame. He was honored by the monarchs of England and Russia, the Royal Geographic Society, and the scientific and maritime societies of Turin and Lisbon. Valdes y Navarrete and von Humboldt corresponded with him concerning this great archive which he was then arranging for final deposit in Spain. After his death Bauza's widow eventually sold the collection to the Venezuelan, Michele y Rojas, who subsequently sold the Bauza Collection to the British Museum. However the Malaspina Expedition drawings went to Spain in 1846. Carlos Sanz Lopez acquired them in 1953 and donated them to the Museo de America in Madrid in 1961. Today we honor all who preserved this priceless archive.

Antonio Pineda, a First Lieutenant in the Guards of the Royal Spanish Infantry, was born in Guatemala in 1753. He was the Expedition naturalist. At the age of six he was sent to Spain, and at seventeen was a cadet in the Guard Corps. In 1780 he served at the Siege of Gibraltar. In addition to skill in mathematics and astronomy he studied botany, chemistry and experimental physics. He also worked with Casimiro Gomez Ortega, Director of the Real Jardin Botanico. Until his death at Badocui in the Philippines, Pineda made keen observations. He studied important volcanoes on both American continents and in the Philippines. He wrote on botany, ethnography, climatography, population, commerce, agriculture, ornithology, zoology, mineralogy and civilizations. He traveled the Mexican interior with botanist Luis Nee and his observations gathered by Jose de Espinosa y Tello were published by Novo y Colson in Madrid in 1885 in the *Viaje.*

One wants to say he was indefatigable, but it would appear he died of fatigue. His associates erected a monument in admiration of his work and love of science in the Botanical Garden of Manila. This was destroyed during World War II.

Jose del Pozo painted landscapes and botanical studies. He was born in Seville in 1757, the son of Pedro del Pozo, Director of the Royal Academy of Painting. Though highly recommended by Francisco de Bruna of Seville, Malaspina was obliged to recognize Pozo's indolent and unproductive personality, and he put him ashore at Callao. Pozo soon founded a very successful painting school in Lima, where he died in 1821. His drawings of Argentina and Chile in the Bauza Collection were acquired through the interest of Bonafacio del Carril and published in 1961.

Antonio Tova y Arredondo was second in command to Bustamante in the *Atrevida*. He was born in 1760 and made midshipman in 1773. He had one year of service in the American Station and was subsequently proposed for the Expedition by Bustamante. He kept a diary of ethnographic and visual interest which was eventually discovered in the municipal library of Santander and published in its incomplete form by San Felini Ortiz.

Dionisio Alcala-Galliano was the subaltern assigned to astronomy. As a midshipman he sailed along the coasts of Brazil and Argentina in 1775, campaigning against the Portugese. In Spain he worked under Tofino on the *Atlas Maritimo* and in 1785 he sailed in the Antonio de Cordoba Expedition to the Straits of Magellan. At 29 he undertook all the astronomical work along the Pacific Coast as far as Acapulco. Alcala-Galliano was the first to establish latitude by means of a polar elevation observed at a certain distance from the meridian (Mendoza y Rios published this finding in 1809). As earlier stated, he was sent north after the return of Malaspina's first Northwest Coast voyage to explore the Strait of Juan de Fuca for a northwest passage in company with Cayetano Valdes. During their exploration of the Strait and the first

circumnavigation of Vancouver Island, they spent much time in nearby waters while Commander Bodega y Quadra and Captain George Vancouver, R.N. were conducting their protracted negotiations at the island then named for them both, Isla de Quadra y Vancouver.

This voyage description was published by the Direccion Hidrografico in 1802 with much interesting ethnographic material by Jose Mozino as well as an illustrated atlas of maps and drawings of which several originals are now in the Bauza Collection. Malaspina is referred to in the account simply as "Commander."

Alcala-Galliano returned to Spain to undertake some naval commissions of a scientific nature. But he took command of the *Bahama* in the Spanish wing of the fleet under command of the French Admiral Villeneuve. Sortying from La Coruna with the combined fleet, he was killed at Trafalgar. His son Antonio Alcola Galliano achieved fame as a political leader and orator.

Juan Gutierrez de la Concha was officer in the department of astronomy. Born in 1760, he served the entire duration of the Expedition but was detached in Montevideo in November 1794 to make a detailed reconnaissance of the Argentine coast.

In 1806 he was decorated by the Spanish government and one year later assigned to the province of Cordoba de Tucuman as Intendant Governor. During the British incursions in Argentina he fought their invasion along the Rio de la Plata. In 1810 he was killed at Cabeza de Tigre when his group of insurgents endeavored to depose the Spanish Governor.

Jose Guio came to the Expedition as

anatomist and painter upon the recommen-
dation of Antonio Pineda. He worked very
productively until Acapulco where he left
for Spain with failing health. There he
worked on Malaspina materials sent on by
his colleagues. Upon effecting a recovery he
sailed for Cuba on the botanical expedition
of the Conde de Monpoxo.

Jose Robredo, *Arcadio Pineda* and
Martin de Olivade were subalterns assigned
to various responsibilities associated with
the formal collection and ordering of scientific findings.

Manuel Esquerra served as accountant;
Francisco de Paula Arreno was chaplain;
Jose Maria Gonzalez, surgeon; *Jacobo
Murphy*, midshipman and *Juan Diaz
Maqueda*, pilot's assistant.

The botanist *Luis Nee*, born in France,
was a naturalized Spanish citizen working in
the Garden of the Priory of the Royal
Apothecary. Malaspina beckoned. Upon
reaching the southern hemisphere, Nee
collected plant materials in Uruguay,
Argentina, Chile, Ecuador and Peru, as well
as the interior of Mexico. In the Philippines
he collected plant life from Luzon and Mindanao and new discoveries were made in
New Holland and Botany Bay. After the
return to Peru he crossed Chile north to
south and then moved east to Mendoza and
the pampas, eventually reaching Buenos
Aires. Making rendezvous with Malaspina
he returned to Spain with his collection.

Other important members were added as
Malaspina found and needed them along his
route, an opportunity not available to
explorers from countries less richly
endowed with colonies and civilized centers
long established as those of Spain's.

Tadeo Haenke, a botanist and naturalist,
joined the *Atrevida* at Valparaiso. The
famous botanist Jacquin had recommended
this Central European protege. Subsequently
accepted, Haenke missed the Cadiz departure. Following along by merchant ship he
met misfortune when the ship was wrecked
near Montevideo. Although he managed to
save himself by swimming, all his baggage
and instruments went down. Viceroy Vertiz
sent him across the pampas and the rugged
Cordillera trail. By the time he reached Santiago and Malaspina the enterprising
botanist had collected 2,500 specimens.

He sailed north with the Expedition to
Callao and explored the interior of Moxas
and Chiquitos. He described the Lagoon of
Chiquito (Lake Titicaca) in detail with
botanist Tafalla and the artist Pulgar.
Throughout the voyage his investigations
were impressive: Ecuador, Panama, Nicaragua, Mexico, Alaska, the islands of
Oceania (especially Guam, the Philippines
and Vavao).

Upon his return to Callao he went off to
examine the Altiplano Andino where for
obscure reasons he decided to settle, in
Cochabamba, Bolivia, and lived there until
his death in 1817. His work during this 23-
year period was frankly monumental,
including 40 cases of botanical and zoologi-
cal specimens he sent to Spain for preservation in his home institutions.

In Peru Malaspina reassigned *Jose
Cardero*, who was serving as an orderly or
perhaps a cabin boy on the *Descubierta*.
He was informally added as a painter-
cartographer for the Expedition when Jose
del Pozo was separated at Callao. His first
rude drawings of record are from

Guayaquil, Nicaragua and Panama. From Mexico north to Alaska the gifted young Spaniard concentrated on natural history interspersed with some individual native and village drawings. Malaspina first recorded that these drawings of "Pepe" Cardero were "those of a simple amateur, not devoid of taste or artistic feeling." Very soon however the simple and accurate drawings of the "amateur" were afforded the recognition and value which ethnographers assign them today.

His unstylized drawings from the first and second northern voyages tell us many things glossed over in the more stylized and finished drawings of his professional superiors. Many scenes sketched from the *Sutil* and *Mexicana* were carried back to Mexico City and worked up at the Academy of San Carlos. They were then taken to Spain for engraving by Fernando Selma for use as the illustrated record for an account of the voyage. After Cardero's return to Spain on the frigate *Minerva*, captained by Cayetano Valdes, he was made a ship's accountant—essentially onshore duty. Eventually he was promoted a lieutenant in naval supply assigned to the Cadiz depot where his name last appears in the Naval Register of 1810.

Jose de Espinosa y Tello came to the *Descubierta* in 1791 at the Acapulco anchorage. Born into a well-known Seville family, Espinosa had worked under the tutelage of Vicente Tofino. He began to officially gather information for the Expedition in 1788, but illness prevented his departure when the ships left Cadiz. On November 25, 1790, he sailed on the *Santa Rosalia* with a companion, Lieutenant Ciriaco Cevallos. He carried to Malaspina the latest naval almanac and other recent publications of interest, no doubt including official news of the latter's promotion to Captain. Mazarredo had also delivered to his care two superb Arnold chronometers, and a longitudinal clock, together with a constant pendulum for simple gravitational experiments. Landing in Cuba, Espinosa moved on to the mainland at Vera Cruz, up to Mexico City and down the long Pacific slope to Acapulco, where he rejoined the Expedition. He sailed with Malaspina to Alaska, Nootka and the Spanish settlements in Oceania. Upon return to South America he left the Expedition at Valparaiso with Bauza and crossed overland to Buenos Aires. In 1794 he returned to Spain and was made Chief of the Direccion de Hidrografia. Among other duties, he oversaw the publication *Relacion de Viaje de las Goletas Sutil y Mexicana* as well as accounts of his own voyages and observations in Chile and Argentina.

Ciriaco Cevallos, who journeyed from Cadiz with Espinosa, was ship's captain. He had achieved distinction in drawing a very precise "Hydrographic chart of the Yucatan peninsula from Campeche Sound and its bays and of the entire length of coast from Vera Cruz to Campeche." He also wrote a conclusive article demonstrating the nonexistence of the fictitious passage which Ferrer Maldonado had persuasively described between the Pacific and Atlantic oceans in 1609.

Tomas de Suria signed on in Mexico. He had left his native city of Madrid and traveled to Mexico City with his painting master Jeronimo Gil. There they founded a school of engraving at the Mint. Viceroy Revillagigedo recommended the young medal maker and engraver to Malaspina and he reached Acapulco on February 16, 1791. In March he was aboard the *Descubierta* working for Pineda, the naturalist. Happily, Suria kept a diary filled with observations about the countryside and the natives he observed. Henry Wagner published this incomplete record in 1936 as did his biographer Justino Fernandez in 1939.

Suria made many portraits of the natives of Port Mulgrave (Yakutat Bay) and Nootka, including detailed scenes of their rites and customs. Upon return to Mexico he was obliged to remain there to work up better delineations of the numerous field sketches. His loss was compensated for by Fernando Brambila and Juan Ravenet, two painters sent expressly to Acapulco from Italy by Malaspina's family friend, the Conde de Greppi.

Suria lived in Mexico until his death, achieving fame in 1805 for his engraving of a commemorative medal honoring Fernando VII.

Fernando Brambila of Milan had accepted a contract for the last part of the voyage. On April 4, 1791, he left Genoa in company with Juan Ravenet and crossed to Spain in order to take passage to Mexico. By November they reached Vera Cruz and crossed Mexico to meet the Expedition returning from the Northwest Coast at Acapulco.

Juan Ravenet had come to the Expedition from Parma. He joined the *Descubierta* at Acapulco and devoted his skill to drawing portraits of typical persons and views in Mexico, Oceania (including Australia), as well as Peru, Chile and the Rio de la Plata. In Spain he worked under Luis Claver at the Academy of San Fernando in the preparation of plates illustrating the voyage.

Aboard the *Atrevida* Brambila drew views of Guam, the Philippines, Macao, Vavao, Peru, Chile and Argentina. In Spain he spent many months preparing his drawings for engraving. He was named Director of Landscape Painting at the Academy of San Fernando and later was attached to the court of Fernando VII. He died in Paris in 1842.

Other members of Malaspina's crew included two pilot's mates, a boatswain and a bloodletter, two boatswain's mates, two cooks, thirteen carpenters, three shipwrights, a blacksmith, diver, cooper and steward, thirty-five naval gunners, ten cabin boys or orderlies, one naval surgeon, two naval corporals, twelve soldiers, three brigade members, seven servants for the commander and officers and one servant for the natural historian. The crew of the *Atrevida*, with 104 persons, was a similar complement.

On May 1, 1791, then, the corvettes left Acapulco each carrying fourteen six-pound cannon, two four-pounders, and eight additional six-pounders in their holds. On June 23 they were north of San Bartolome which Bodega y Quadra had examined in 1775, James Cook in 1778, and Captain George Dixon, R.N. had verified in 1786. On the 25th they sighted Cabo del Buen Tiempo (Cape Edgecumbe ?) and in Bering Bay Malaspina decided to move northeast through the long daylight to explore Mulgrave (Yakutat) Sound.

Near the entrance to Yakutat an opening in the mountain range was observed. Could this actually be the Maldonado passage? A surprised excitement reigned. They moved into Mulgrave (Yakutat) surrounded by dramatically decorated natives singing chants of peace and welcome, or so it seemed at the time. Troubles with these awesome Tlingits would come later, especially for the Russian fur traders. Anchoring in a beautiful location, the crews noted the snow covered mountain ranges, hills clothed with conifers, and the curious Indians offering fresh water, furs and exotic objects from their culture. The observatory tent was taken to a stable point on land where accurate positions were fixed, and the chronometers reset. Not only was latitude determined, but Mount St. Elias and other peaks were measured for height. "A great mountain range which is constantly covered with snow on its slopes forms the entire coast from the Monte de la Cruz to the extreme east of Cook Inlet. It is hard to believe that even in the months of June and July these mountains are covered with snow and. . .are destined to be forever inhabited only by bears."

Two cutters were prepared for a 15-day exploration of the inlet, but very shortly the party met floating ice and then a frozen ice barrier denoting a giant glacier. While Port Mulgrave, named for a British Lord of the Admiralty, was eventually discarded as a name, the giant ice mass was later named Malaspina Glacier. Although disappointed in the inlet, as denoted by "Bahia del Desengano" ("bay of detected error") the intellectually curious leader spent many days in the Yakutat Bay recording, measur-

ing, exploring, drawing; describing all aspects of the unknown land in the very best Encyclopedist tradition. As time went on the Indians became more bold and acquisitive and problems developed because of petty thievery and bodily handling. But these tense confrontations allowed the artists and scientists ever more opportunity to describe the complicated culture of the powerful northern villages and tribes. After sailing north to Hinchinbrook Island (near the present town of Cordova), the Expedition ceased collecting among the savage Chugach and turned south on July 27. On August 12 they approached Nootka at sunset. A launch from the Spanish corvette *Concepcion* came out to meet them and in the morning they entered Friendly Cove (Cala de los Amigos or Santa Cruz de Nuca in Spanish) to the salutes of cannon mounted in the already famous Fort San Miguel, the recently emplaced fortification of Nootka.

Esteban Martinez, a familiar northern traveler, had been instructed to fortify the site to frustrate Russian and English intentions. He had arrived on May 5, 1789, with orders to treat the Indians with every consideration and to build barracks and entrenchments. Of course the site chosen had been an Indian summer campground from time immemorial. Impetuous Martinez had since departed and in his diary Malaspina noted that Francisco Elisa was in command, while Ramon Saavedra commanded the *Concepcion* and Pedro Alberni headed a crack company of Catalonian infantry formerly stationed in the Southwest, and probably used against the Apaches.

Malaspina noted: "in the depth of the

port could be seen various dwellings built of planks; Alberni watched over them vigilantly and kept all in order with the troops billeted on land; fresh bread was baked [daily]." He commented on "the cultivation of the gardens on which Nature had already lavished her gifts; the care of the provisions and defense equipment."

The natives such as could be seen "were not unlike other Americans [natives] who live on this continent, except that those in Nootka have a head in a pyramidal shape, which is no doubt due to the fact that when they are born, and before they are placed in little oblong cradles, their heads are shaped with strong ligatures which reach down almost to their eyes." Malaspina went on to say: "They have a custom that when the child is an infant they pierce three or four openings in the lower part of the ears and one or two in the cartilage of the nose." He suggests the matter of cannibalism, a historical fact that most scholars accept today.

Juan Jose Perez, a pilot on an official voyage of exploration, had first come along the coast in 1774. The former Manila galleon pilot had with him as second another pilot of less experience, Esteban Jose Martinez. They had sailed north in the *Santiago* in January of 1775. On their southern return from approximately 50° north latitude, Perez sighted Vancouver Island, and August 8, 1792, he was in the roadstead (Surgidero de San Lorenzo) of Nootka. Thus he was the first European recorded at the famous anchorage, but it would seem Captain Cook was first to sail inside the sound, and to the cove which he named Friendly Harbor before the displaced

Indians began to show their deeper feelings. Of course we know that Captain Cook had named the large sound after King George and eventually he called the inlet Nookka and finally Nootka, which is not a recognizable Indian word. And now 16 years after the first visit Friendly Cove (Santa Cruz de Nuca) was an important and highly controversial settlement known in every European embassy.

The Malaspina party immediately moved their observatories ashore and notes were taken about the much enlarged outpost. The natives were invited to parley with Malaspina as well as the local commanders, Pedro Alberni and Ramon Saavedra. The negotiations were as usual complex. The villages were involved in their own struggles for power among the tribes and individual chiefs—not to mention the surely confusing European rivalries, with occasional contributions by American merchant traders such as Robert Gray and William Kendrick. But scientific inquiry was assisted by the fact that in Nootka there were persons to interpret the questions as well as the answers.

On an exploratory voyage by cutter, Espinosa and Cevallos concluded that the inhabitants in the island complex numbered no more than 4,000—that is, those under the suzerainty of the aged chief Macuina. They also made a rough chart of the Bay of Buena Esperanza. "The land which comprises the archipelago is altogether singular. There are as many as five channels or arms not generally wider than a third of a mile, penetrating in different directions, ending in several small coves or bays chosen by the natives for their settlements." They returned to Malaspina on August 25, 1791. Macuina then consented to come aboard the *Descubierta* for tea, of which he had several cups. "On his head he wore a kind of band of scarlet cloth in which were fastened some little glass stars. . .the scarcity of food had made him very weak and thin. . . whereas earlier many had remarked on his strength and dexterity, to the point where he would singlehandedly harpoon a whale."

On the 28th the two ships moved slowly out of the tricky harbor carrying with them twenty children who had been variously purchased in order to save them from being eaten by their Indian captors or owners. Malaspina was bound for the Entrada de Hezeta, reported by the *Santiago* in 1775 and not seen since. Malaspina's intention in all these sightings, profile drawings and landings, was to better formalize locations and to establish the fact that they were unoccupied lands properly claimed by the King of Spain. However a summer fog obscured the coast where the (Columbia) river mouth was thought to be and Malaspina proceeded south toward Monterey. Captain Robert Gray of Boston would take possession of the elusive "River of the West" (Entrada de Hezeta) the following spring, further frustrating Spanish colonial designs.

Fog prevailed in Monterey as well. Cannon fire was used to guide the Expedition to a safe anchorage at the Presidio on September 11, 1791. The tents were landed, and many collections gathered and described in close detail. The artists' drawings reveal that while it was more familiar and pleasant, life was less theatrical than with the primitive tribesmen of the north.

On September 26 the captains moved away from the beautiful harbor to their prearranged revictualing in Acapulco.

Atrevida completed a survey begun earlier of the waters between Cape Corriente and Acapulco, then Bustamante rejoined Malaspina in port. After working out arrangements for the now obviously necessary second Northwest Coast expedition of the two small draft schooners *Sutil* and *Mexicana* built in San Blas, Malaspina sailed west for the Marianas (visited earlier by Spanish explorers Marquina, Ayeusa and Sanchez). Although Malaspina had to write off his Hawaiian Islands trip, he did correct the position of the Cape of San Bartolome, discovered in the days of cruder navigational aids by Alonso de Salazar. Explorations of Guam and the Carolines were followed by visits to the Philippine ports of Palapag, Sorsogon and Manila. Mapping was done on the islands of Luzon, Mindoro, Mindanao and Negros.

Atrevida cruised in the China Sea as far as Formosa and Portuguese Macao below Canton. Gathering surveys and specimens they moved south to Espiritu Santo and the area of Dusky Sound in New Zealand, so well described in Cook's earlier travel accounts. The course was then to Sydney, Australia, up to the Friendly (Tonga) Islands, then south to the 50th parallel. Sailing to 80° longitude west of the meridian of San Fernando, Chile, they moved in almost a circle route north to Callao. After further observations on the Peruvian coastline Malaspina turned south again, rounding the Horn far away from the Straits of Magellan. Passing the Islas Malvinas and the Aurora Islands they reached the South Atlantic and

Montevideo, the last rendezvous for scattered Expedition members.

Homeward bound at last, the Expedition crossed the Atlantic approximately following the 20th west meridian to raise the Azores and then northeast to Cadiz. When they arrived September 21, 1793, a five-year voyage of immense scientific benefit as well as a superb feat of seamanship was at last completed. The officers and crew had performed up to their commander's best expectations, but so also had the scientists and learned men who had so generously given of themselves during the five-year "pursuit of knowledge." Although Malaspina had received his captaincy belatedly he was immediately advanced to Brigadier (Rear Admiral).

Antonio Valdes, the head of naval affairs, could take pride in his original statement issued with the appointment of the able Parmese officer: "By reason of his knowledge, his family, the nobility and elegance of his person and his manners, his self-assured presence, affability, firmness of character and talent in moving in society, Malaspina was foremost in our armada, and the only one for that command; he was the very essence of the cultured and distinguished society which our seamen must represent in the American lands in order to have a favorable influence on the Creoles and aid and consummate the policy which the Expedition demanded." As witness of this original judgment King Carlos IV issued a royal decree March 17, 1795, expressing his high regard for the accomplishments of Malaspina and his men. He ordered his commander to come to court to render a personal account of his feat.

From that point everything began to go downhill.

An interesting point is that the atmosphere in the ships seems to have been for the most part harmonious as well as physically healthy. Considering the number of Expedition members who later voluntarily left Spain, or who were sent away, or who fought for increased liberty in the colonies or in other countries, one can suppose the shipboard atmosphere was disciplined but full of liberal ideas. In their many visits around South America to the chief cities in the Spanish colonial world, Malaspina and his companions may have encountered what is today referred to as the problem of *americanismo*, and the suddenly developing sense in the colonies of becoming American rather than being Spanish. German Anciniegas refers to this as the new self awareness.

Von Humboldt later remarked, "the Creoles prefer to be called Americans. . .they are frequently heard to declare with pride, 'I am not a Spaniard, I am an American!'" Malaspina might easily have absorbed some germs of this attitude, for he too was a nationalist from an ancient but conquered territory—Parma.

It is suggested that Malaspina perceived a new nationalism being fanned in part by the Jesuits recently exiled from Europe. He sensed it and was impressed, not only by the nationalistic desires but also by resentments. It is this aspect of Malaspina's voyage that is the most interesting of all—as an intellectual carrier between two complex worlds and two vast oceans.

Whenever or however it occurred Malaspina returned home a committed and enthusiastic liberal, at least by the standards of the too trusting monarch and his principal henchman, the corrupt young dragoon Manuel Godoy (now referred to as a statesman and eventually the "Prince of Peace"— a serious misnomer).

It appears that Malaspina may have been somewhat worn out with fatigue, which would be perfectly understandable, and perhaps out of touch with reality. He showed symptoms of Cook's malaise after too many unendurable strains. In working up his report of the voyage with Father Gil, a minor cleric of Seville, Malaspina had developed his original philosophical thoughts, which had blossomed into ideas too advanced if not inimical to his royal patrons. Essentially he espoused freedom for the South American colonies; he favored tax exemptions, franchises for navigation, commerce and agriculture, a duty free port in Spain for foreign commerce and other concessions. Although he wished to "conserve the unity of the systems of religion, laws and the military within the metropolis," he was working in dark and dangerous waters.

Many powerful persons were distressed with the situation of the Spanish court, one which Francisco de Goya had painted all too accurately. Carlos IV (1788-1805) was a pale shadow of his powerful father Carlos III, who had reigned 29 years. In a time of rebellious feelings everywhere, when Britain in fact had lost much of her holdings, Carlos III had made Spain more powerful than ever abroad. But his inadequate son soon received rough treatment from Pitt in Great Britain, and then from France. His father's internal reforms atro-

phied, the vigorous Queen's ambitious lover Godoy rose to power and once significant advisers complained bitterly. Many decried the loss of Louisiana to France, the corruption and the general conduct of the mercurial and sensual Queen, and Spain's stumbling decline in European affairs. There were those who perhaps saw in Malaspina an opportunity to dislodge Godoy, now fully astride the affections of both King and Queen. But it was not to be. Malaspina could never have outmaneuvered the polished thug Godoy, who despite his tireless greed had even more to gain. And Godoy's inclinations were sensual, not romantic.

The Italian ambassador to Spain, Conde de Greppi, was a family friend of Malaspina's, and perhaps even a plotter in this instance. He described the situation thus: "this voyage has made a deep impression on [Malaspina's] passionate soul as to what is best for his fellow creatures, thinking of the absolute necessity for a radical change in the system of government and for legislation in the colonies. . .he insists on the necessity of removing as many hindrances as possible to free development, seeking to unite that empire with fuller and more reciprocal relations." The ambassador's account continued: "in the midst of these arguments he admitted that he was somewhat hot-headed, but was still sufficiently prudent to comprehend that it had been most inappropriate to expound upon his project on such an occasion. He lost sight of the fact that this idea was his downfall."

Certainly these were dangerous thoughts in absolutist Spain, beset with ancient problems as well as the tyrannies, large and small, of Godoy's followers. But more, it would seem that Malaspina became entangled through political writings involving Spain and France, especially the recently concluded treaty with the new republic engineered by the "Prince of Peace." The final blow, however, might be the possibility that the dashing and impetuous Malaspina of the "full lips," "eyes. . .expressive," and "nose. . .generous and flaring," had eclipsed Godoy in the affections of the earthy Bourbon Maria Luisa, daughter of the Duke of Parma, and Queen to sluggish Carlos IV. Unfortunately, whatever the degree of the intrigue, Malaspina with his passion for planning, wrote everything down. While one of the aggressive Queen's ladies-in-waiting, La Matallana, favored Malaspina's political plans, another favored the continued success of Godoy. The "plan," which was theoretically secure in the Queen's possession, was very soon being analyzed by Godoy and Carlos IV. On the night of November 23, 1795, Admiral Malaspina was arrested, indicted, and restricted to the barracks of the Life Guards; then later sent to the prison castle in the bay of La Coruna, exiled and stripped of all office and rank. La Matallana too was banished from court. An expectant public waiting for the descriptive volumes promised from the illustrious voyage waited in vain. A state trial against Malaspina and

Father Gil was eventually abandoned, and several years later the Admiral was banished from Spain.

Aside from Malaspina's personal disaster another profound tragedy was the eventual breakup of the magnificent archival treasures he had brought together, for the published account of the voyage was planned from the beginning to rival the great achievements of France and Great Britain in activities where Spain had to her detriment been much too secretive. In Lombardy, far from "his country," Malaspina worked in obscurity with the problems of yellow fever and other troubling afflictions. On April 9, 1810 he died (one hopes not in obscure disquietude) in the village of Pontremoli, a 55-year-old unsung hero whom his admirer von Humboldt too well described: "this able navigator is more famous for his misfortunes than for his discoveries."

When accounts of his voyage and explorations were published his name was not mentioned, and if note was taken Malaspina was referred to simply as "Commander." But now, at last, perhaps with justice, because of our pursuits of knowledge and as a result of modern Spanish scholarship and the energies focused in the bicentennial of the American Revolution, Admiral Alejandro Malaspina is coming to an estimable place in the annals of magnificent voyages.

THE BAUZA COLLECTION IN THE MUSEO DE AMERICA, MADRID

In 1961 the Museo de America in Madrid received a collection of 172 original drawings including maps, views, portraits and customs of America, Asia and Oceania, all done by artists who had accompanied the Malaspina Expedition.

The collection was given to the Museum by a distinguished patron of the arts, Carlos Sanz Lopez. He had acquired the collection from one of the descendants of Felipe Bauza, the director of charts and plans and the chief artist of the Expedition.

The scholarly world had not known about these drawings, although they were known by the preservationists in the Museo Naval of Madrid, which had grown from the defunct Direccion de Hidrografia. In 1951 Guillermo Amar de la Torre, who was married to a granddaughter of Bauza, showed them to the Director of the Museo Naval, Julio Guillen, who organized an exhibition of the drawings. The successful exposition was repeated a year later in the Casa Colon in Las Palmas on the Canary Islands, including a brief catalog of the drawings selected.

The collection was then returned to its owner. He decided to sell it, and in 1953 Bonifacio del Carril bought the drawings pertaining to Chile and Argentina, while Carlos Sanz bought the rest, with the exception of four maps, six views of the island of Vavao and some of Australia. Fortunately in 1961 the Spanish government was able to acquire the Vavao maps and drawings and deposit them in the Museo de America where they again became part of the collection. The whereabouts of the drawings of Australia are presently unknown.

Most of the drawings are unsigned, except for those done by Cardero and two by Ravenet; but it is possible to attribute most of the drawings to individual artists because there are examples of their work preserved in the collection of the Museo Naval in Madrid. The painter Suria also illustrated his diary with sketches as well as notes found in the account of the voyage enriched with the diaries of Viana and Antonio Tova. Most of the views were prepared for engraving, and in spite of the fact that they are not signed, they are believed to be the work of Fernando Brambila.

The drawings which Cardero made of the Strait of Juan de Fuca were later engraved by Fernando Selma of the Academy of San Fernando to illustrate the Atlas of the *Relacion* published by the Direccion de Hidrografia in 1802.

The Museo de America collection does not include the drawings of Chile and Argentina, and the most important items are the drawings of the Northwest Coast and of the Marianas and Philippines.

At present the Bauza Collection is exhibited in a special gallery in the Museo de America, along with ethnological artifacts from the same expedition formerly housed in the Real Gabinete de Historia Natural.

THE
PICTORIAL
RECORD

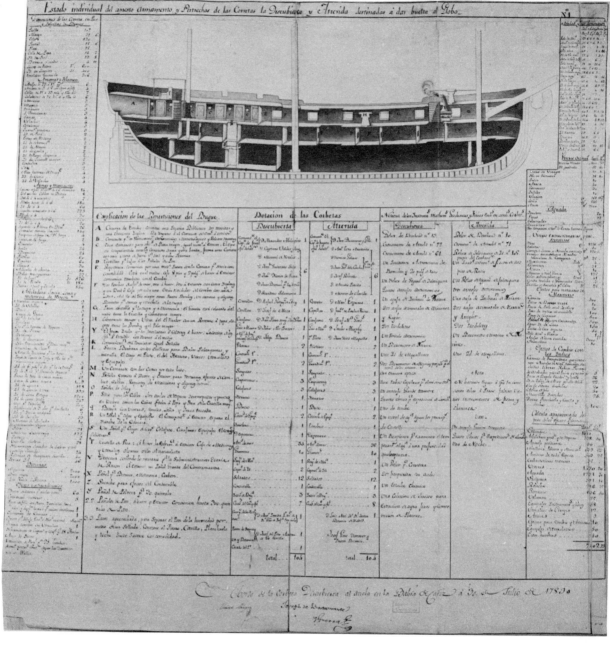

1 Ferdinand Bauza, *Accourtrement, armament and defense equipment of the corvettes* Descubierta *and* Atrevida, *which are to sail around the world.*
Inscription: "Estado individual del apresto, armamento y pertrechos de las corvetas la Descubierta y Atrevida, destinadas a dar buelta al globo."
Museo de America Coll. (Bauza No. 1).

Ferdinand Bauza's illustration of the cross-section of the twin corvettes *Descubierta* and *Atrevida*, with accompanying lists of dimensions, equipment, supplies, descriptions of the various parts of the vessels, and a list of the members of both the officer corps and crew of each ship, provides a unique, preserved record practically without comparison. This single illustration tells the modern student of history almost more about the Malaspina Expedition than any other single document or illustration that has remained to our day.

The enlightened scientific quality of the Malaspina Expedition began with the planning for the exploration. This cutaway, and accompanying lists reveal a scientific thoroughness that pervaded the voyages.

The column on the left gives the "Dimensions of the Corvettes in *pies* (1 *pie* = .91 feet) and *pulgadas* (1 *pulgada* = .076 feet)," and names the "Hawsers and Sails" ("Amarras y Velamen"), "Arms and Munitions," a list of "Masts and Spars, Tackle, Canvas and Pulley blocks" ("Arboladura, Jarcia, Lona y motoneria de Respecto"), the "Tars" ("betunes") carried on the ships, and a miscellany of "Odd Goods" ("efectos extraordinarios"). In the latter list we find a "portable observatory."

The second column lists the various compartments of the hull ("EXPLICACION DE LAS REPARTICIONES DEL BUQUE") and gives a full explanation of the division of the ship.

The next column, "Complement ("Dotacion") of the corvettes" cites the officers and more important men by position and name; the number of crewmen in lesser positions is also given.

Subdivided column four gives an itemized list of "geodesic and physical instruments" by ship, with an interesting note at the beginning of the *Atrevida* list:

The orders sent to Paris were not received on time and therefore certain physical and chemical equipment is missing.

The last, and right-hand, column notes provisions, water and clothing on board the two ships at the start of the voyage. The section "Efectos de Cambio con Los Yndios" ("Items for exchange with the Indians"), a list of the weights of all items on board (including the men), and "Unusual provisions and preservatives" ("Viveres extraordinarios y preservativos") complete the last column.

2 Archivo General de Indias Coll.

An important early map showing the North Pacific Ocean with a general description of the voyages of discovery and exploration for that period, including those of Vitus Bering and Aleksei Chirikov in 1741 and Bodega y Quadra and Francisco Antonio Mourelle in 1775. This 1779 (?) watercolor drawing from the Archivo General de Indias in Seville is remarkable for its color and demonstrates the amount of information known at that time and indicates many unknown and uncharted coasts and islands.

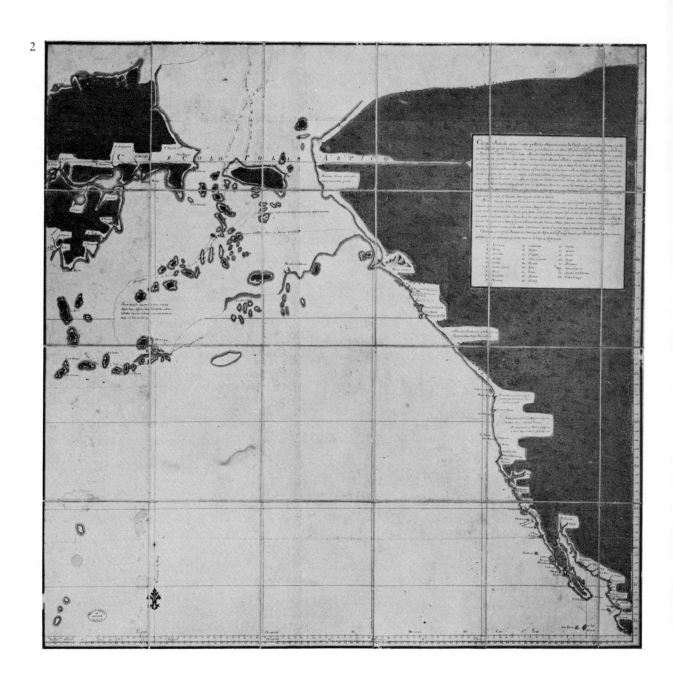

2

22 / VOYAGES OF ENLIGHTENMENT

3 Archivo General de Indias Coll.

This important 1750 map, published by the Imperial Academy of Sciences in St. Petersburg, was sent to Spain in 1764 along with a 207-page report concerning Russian penetration of the North Pacific. The report which included news of Joseph Billings' recent voyage was unsettling, and the reaction was substantial. The map noted in detail the voyages of sailors in the Russian Imperial Service and was viewed with alarm by the Spanish, as was the voyage and nomenclature of Francis Drake so generously entered at New Albion along with the fact of his 1579 encampment.

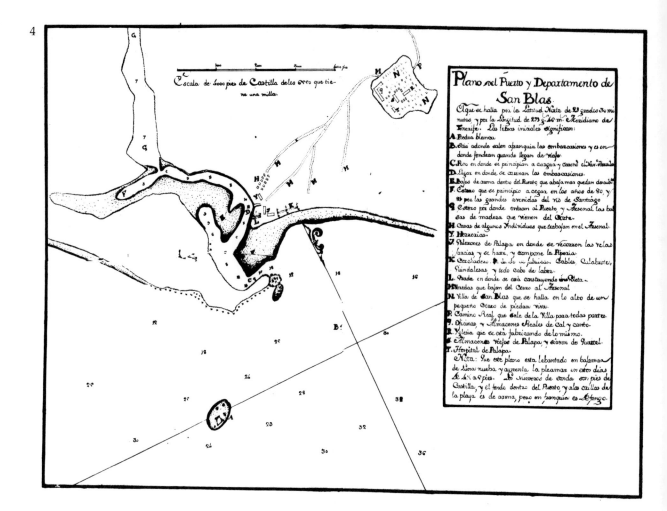

4 Archivo General de Indias Coll.

This beautifully drawn plan (1791) shows the ill-sited port and installations of San Blas some years after its first location (about 55 sailing days from Lima's port, Callao) by Spanish administrators in 1767. Malaspina's second in command Bustamante gave the malaria-infested port a low rating in its swamp-surrounded location.

Most extraordinary was the magnificent record achieved in the shipyards of this advanced supply station, including the expediting of materials other than hardwoods which abounded in the region. A sheltered harbor with a bar that constantly shifted, yet the 82-foot, 225-ton *Santiago* (first to sight the Columbia River mouth in 1775) was launched and outfitted here in 1773. At its height about 750 persons were employed in the yards, with a town population of 20,000 in 1791.

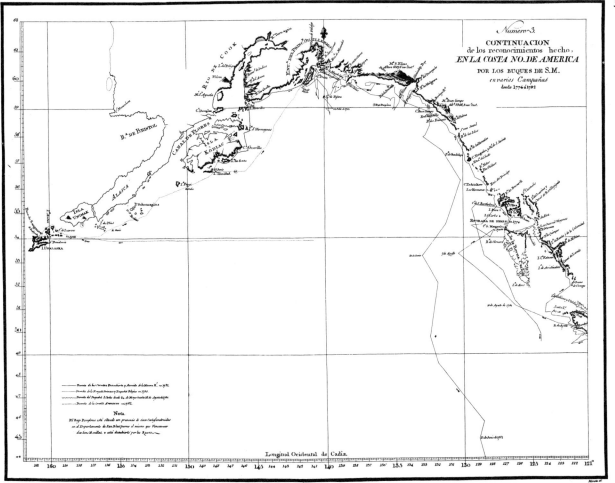

5 Museo Naval Coll.

A full view of the Gulf of Alaska, from the Aleutians to the northern tip of Vancouver Island (at right margin), indicates the route (solid line) of the *Descubierta* and *Atrevida* between the 15th of June and the 11th of August, 1791. Other lines indicate explorations in this area between 1774 and 1792.

MALASPINA ON THE NORTHWEST COAST / 25

6

6 Museo Naval Coll.

Copy of the original rough chart of the northern-
most journey of the corvettes, showing Admiralty Bay and the Port of Mulgrave (Yakutat).
The rocky inlet south of Mount St. Elias, the
"icy bay" where Malaspina Glacier obstructed
the explorers, may be seen today.

26 / VOYAGES OF ENLIGHTENMENT

7 [Tomas de Suria or Felipe Bauza], *The corvettes "Descubierta" and "Atrevida" and a view of Mount St. Elias* [Alaska]. Inscription: "Corbetas 'Descubierta' y vista de [San Elias?]." Museo de America Coll. (Bauza No. 5). Pencil and wash sketch on canvas. 43 x 27 cm.

The sketch shows in the foreground the two corvettes, and in the background a snow-covered mountain, which we believe to be Mount St. Elias. In de Suria's *Diario* he refers to various drawings made on the 24th, 25th and 26th of June, 1791. This may be one of them, with *Descubierta* on the left.

MALASPINA ON THE NORTHWEST COAST / 27

8 Juan Ravenet, *View of Port Desengano*.
Inscription: "Vista del Puerto del Desengano en
Lat^d de 59°45'." Museo Naval Coll. (Ms.
1726-73). Watercolor and white pastel. 71.5 x
48 cm.

Here is the "icy bay" to which Malaspina, Antonio Tova and Felipe Bauza journeyed, accompanied by a son of An-Kau, in search of the
Maldonado passage to the Atlantic Ocean. Geo-
detic surveys were made, maps drawn and a
massive [Malaspina] glacier noted. The first
sketch for this may have been made by Cardero, but we know that both Ravenet and
Brambila had Malaspina's permission to "im-
prove" Cardero's drawings. It was not unusual
for recording artists to later borrow from one
another; Brambila's famous engravings of "Puente
del Inca," "Rindos de Bustos," and "El Callejon"
were all taken from sketches by Bauza.

9 Jose Cardero, *View of Port Mulgrave* [Yakutat Bay]. Inscription: "Vista del alojamiento de los Indios y del Puerto de Mulgrabe sacada desde su bajo." Museo de America Coll. (Bauza No. 9). Watercolor. 33.3 x 48.6 cm.

In this drawing Cardero has represented in great detail the corvettes *Descubierta* and *Atrevida* anchored in Port Mulgrave [Yakutat] (named by Captain Dixon), where they put in on June 27, 1791, to reconnoitre a gorge, hoping that they might find there the transcontinental passage described by Lorenzo Ferrer Maldonado. They explored the gorge and found a very short channel filled with ice. They named this place Bahia del Desengano, "Bay of Detected Error."

The view is well composed, and was probably done by Cardero under the direction of the artist Brambila, who joined the Expedition in Acapulco when the corvettes returned. The penant on the sloop at the right suggests that this is Malaspina's flagship. Since the sailors on shore are washing their clothes this may be where the famous pants were lost.

10   Jose Cardero, *The Chief of Mulgrave asks
     peace from the corvettes.* Inscription: "Cacique
     de Mulgrave pidiendo la paz a las Corbetas."
     Museo de America Coll. (Bauza No. 50).
     Colored wash, 26.3 x 36.3 cm.

This meticulously executed drawing by Cardero
is rich in ethnographic details. It shows another
scene in the sequence of events which occurred
on July 5. The Chief had been detained aboard
the *Atrevida* in order to prevent an attack
which could have been fatal. This was a formal
procedure developed earlier by James Cook.
The natives offer the sailor's pants they had
cleverly stolen, in exchange for peace.

30 / VOYAGES OF ENLIGHTENMENT

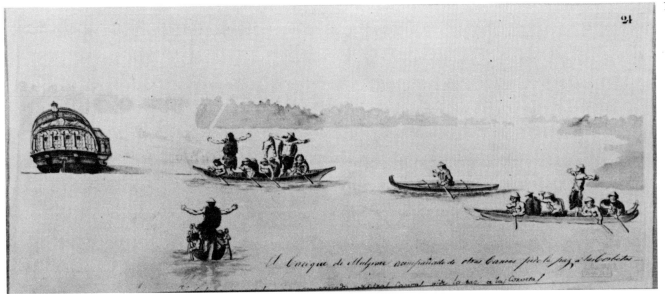

11 [Jose Cardero], *The Chief of Mulgrave in his canoe, accompanied by two additional canoes, with arms open as a sign of peace to the corvettes.* Inscription: "El Cacique de Mulgrave acompanado de otras Canoas pide la paz a las Corbetas." Museo de America Coll. (Bauza No. 24). Watercolor sketch. 17.3 x 40.2 cm.

This sketch, which includes a handsome stern gallery view and a northern hunting baidarka, shows the final incident of July 5, 1791, when a series of events resulted in an Indian attack. An Indian had stolen a pair of breeches from one of the sailors, and in reprisal all barter was halted. The open arms indicate the Indians ask for peace. The Chief's canoe shown in the drawing follows Cardero, for which reason we attribute it to him, although it could have been done by de Suria. The Spanish reports do not convey the ferocity of the Tlingits, the tribe which Russian traders and officials soon found unconquerable.

MALASPINA ON THE NORTHWEST COAST / 31

12 [Tomas de Suria or Felipe Bauza], *Attack by the Indians of Port Mulgrave.* Inscription: "Escena en el Puerto de Mulgrave." Museo de America Coll. (Bauza No. 22). Wash sketch, 24.7 x 44.1 cm.

The sketch represents the events which occurred on July 5, 1791, between the natives of Port Mulgrave and the officers of the corvettes. Officer Juan Bernacci asked for help, and a cannon shot was fired by the *Descubierta* at right; meanwhile Jose de Espinosa y Tello and four armed soldiers landed on the beach to settle the situation. The drawing is tentatively attributed to de Suria by the Museo de America, but it may have been done by Bauza. In the background the scientists seem to be packing up.

13 Jose Cardero, *A structure in Port Mulgrave.* Inscription: "Casa de Inbierno sin techo en el Puerto de Mulgrave." Museo de America Coll. (Bauza No. 10). Watercolor. 30.8 x 42.5 cm.

This drawing, in spite of the inscription at the bottom, has confused any number of persons. Novo y Colson remarks: "Don Tomas de Suria has made a perspective view showing the posts and beams which enclose a large dwelling prepared for winter." The description appears to correspond to this drawing, but not the name of the artist, since we know this was done by Cardero. Probably the shaped timbers of awesome size, so highly valued by the house owners, were floated off to the summer dwelling. They were sometimes conveyed across several canoes

like the example in the water behind the explorers, and they were handed down through families, sometimes several generations.

14 [Tomas de Suria], *Portrait of an Indian of Mulgrave*. Inscription: "Mulgrave." Museo de America Coll. (Bauza No. 103). Pencil drawing. 20 x 15 cm.

We see a rather striking young woman with slanted eyes and prominent cheekbones, not without beauty. She wears an ornament in her nose, probably of bone (although some used nails). This enigmatic portrait is unfinished, but

reveals the hand of an artist. The inscription appears to have been written by de Suria.

15 Jose Cardero, *Hat of the Mulgrave Chief*. Inscription: "Sombrero o Turbante del Gefe de Mulgrawe." Museo de America Coll. (Bauza No. 81). Watercolor. 25.2 x 17.6 cm.

In the Ethnographic Section of the Museo de America several wooden hat rims similar to this one have been preserved, but they are missing the upper part. Of superb design, carved and painted, these Tlingit headpieces are seldom found intact with the woven basketry rings

14

15

16

17

rising from the opening at the top. They were apt to be decorated with more verve in the north than in the more southerly regions.
16

[Tomas de Suria], *Portrait of a Mulgrave woman holding an infant in a cradle.* Pencilled inscription on reverse: "Indio de Mulgrave." Museo de America Coll. (Bauza No. 70). Pencil. 31.2 x 22.2 cm.

A woman sitting with her legs doubled under her holds an infant in a cradle. The woman's lower lip is enlarged by a labret, a usual practice for married women, and the child's nose has been pierced. In the *Diario* of de Suria there is reproduced a rough sketch of a woman holding an infant in its cradle, and another showing details of a woman with a lip disc and pierced nose; both may have been used by the artist as models for this finished drawing prepared for possible engraving.
17

[Tomas de Suria], *An Indian of Mulgrave.*

Inscription: "Mulgrave." Museo de America Coll. (Bauza No. 113). Pen and wash. 21 x 9.8 cm.

A Tlingit of Mulgrave, covered with a heavy pelt, probably a bearskin. He wears a woven hat and in his right hand holds a doublebladed fighting knife made of iron, with a richly ornamented handle and rawhide grip. This is probably a drawing of the Indian who during the events of July 5, 1791, drew his dagger and threatened Lieutenant Cayetano Valdes.
18

[Tomas de Suria], *Portrait of Macuina.* Inscription: "Gefe de Nutka." Museo de America Coll. (Bauza No. 37). Pencil. 18.3 x 12.5 cm.

This superb portrait of Nootka chief Macuina is attributed to de Suria, since a very similar one in the Museo Naval bears his signature. Of unpredictable disposition, Macuina could be fierce, suspicious and intrepid in rapid succession. It was noted that his body did not correspond to

Natzapi de Nutka

Mujer de Nutka

18   19   20

his dignity, for he was short, withered and had nervous mannerisms. This drawing has great historical interest because of the importance of this chief, and because of the so perfectly depicted ethnographic details of his hat, clothing, ornamentation and physical features. In 1778 Cook described them thus: "Their cloaths are made of skins of land and sea animals, in the making of which there is very little of either art or trouble. . . . For a head dress they have a strong straw hat which is shaped like a flowerpot and is as good a covering for the head as can possibly be invented. Thus cloathed, with sometimes the addition of a Coarse Mat over all, they sit in their Canoes in the heaviest rain as unconcerned as we can under the best cover."

19 [Tomas de Suria], *Portrait of Natzapi, brother-in-law of Macuina.* Inscription: "Natzapi de Nutka." Museo de America Coll. (Bauza No. 69). Pencil. 29.1 x 19.9 cm.

This exceptional portrait is probably an unfinished work of de Suria, revealing not only important features but a personality and spirit. In the account of the voyage there are various references to Natzapi: ". . .during the last days the corvettes lingered in the port [of Nootka], we had the pleasure of becoming acquainted with the two brothers Nanikius and Natzapi, brothers-in-law of Macuina, the second eventually the widower of the daughter of Chief Nuchimas. . . . In their eyes, their demeanor, their inclination toward friendship with the Europeans, and the ease with which these two brothers can understand and make themselves understood lets one perceive such perspicacity, and a character so human and a gentle receptivity to new ideas. . .that they could become the reformers of these settlements with the help of the Europeans." These were the men who furnished the Expedition with most of the data pertaining to Nootka Archipelago, Chief Macuina, the description of the region, life and

customs and the penal code.

20 [Tomas de Suria], *Portrait of Natzapi's wife.*
Inscription: "Muger de Nutka." Museo de
America Coll. (Bauza No. 68). Pencil. 29.2 x
21.5 cm.

In the "Indice" to the album of Bauza drawings
this sketch is described along with that of Natzapi as "two pencil portraits of Natzapi and his
wife—Nootka." We know that Natzapi was the
widower of the daughter of the Chief, Nuchimas; but we have no information on this
woman. It is possible that the "Indice" is mistaken and that this may be a portrait of some
other woman of the same tribe, or that she was
Natzapi's second wife, a common custom among
the Nootka chiefs, who might take as many as
three wives.

21 [Fernando Brambila], *View of a natural
corridor on the Northwest Coast of America.*
Inscription: "Vista de la Costa en el Estrecho
Mulgrave con una galeria natural—Costa NO.
de America." Museo de America Coll. (Bauza
No. 36). Finished drawing for engraving. 58 x
33.5 cm.
The drawing shows a kind of natural corridor
covered with a romantic canopy of vegetation
which does not correspond to known vegetation
at Yakutat or Nootka. It was engraved by
Maura and reproduced in Novo y Colson's
book in 1885, ascribed to Brambila, after a
sketch by either de Suria or Cardero. The mistaken plate reads: "View of a natural gallery 100
feet long and 10 wide, in the region of Puerto
del Descanso, in the strait of Juan de Fuca." The
gallery may have been carved by heavy tides
and the classically proportioned natives may
reveal something now lost from view.

36 / VOYAGES OF ENLIGHTENMENT

22 [Unattributed], *Portrait of a Nootka Chief and his wife*. Inscription: "Yndia e Yndio, Gefes de Nutka." Museo de America Coll. (Bauza No. 96). Ink. 21.5 x 13.5 cm.

This shows a man and a woman of the "Tais" ruling class. The woman wears a cape over one shoulder, probably woven of cedar bark which was typical of the clothing of the Nootkas; the man wears a fur cape, perhaps of sea otter, moose or bear, and the classic pear topped hat featuring whale hunting designs worn only by chiefs. We do not know which Nootka chief is portrayed here, but in the Library of the Ministerio de Asuntos Exteriores in Madrid, Manuscript 146, No. 30, shows a figure drawn by N. Moncayo, with the inscription "Tais de Nutca," similar to this one. Manuscript No. 33 also includes a drawing by Marchena with the inscription "Taisa de Nutca." Marchena and Moncayo, students of the Academy of San Carlos in Mexico, may have copied the originals, supposed to have been done by de Suria, Cardero or especially by Anastasio Echevarria.

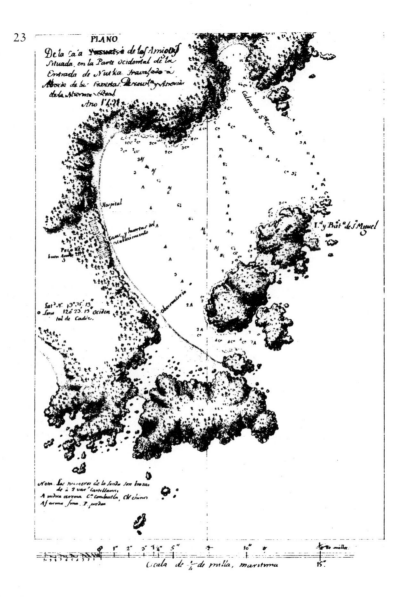

23 Museo Naval Coll.

Nootka: Plan of Friendly Cove drawn aboard
Malaspina's corvettes shows the hospital, "pozo"
(or well) and battery; it describes the habitations
as "houses and huts of the settlement."

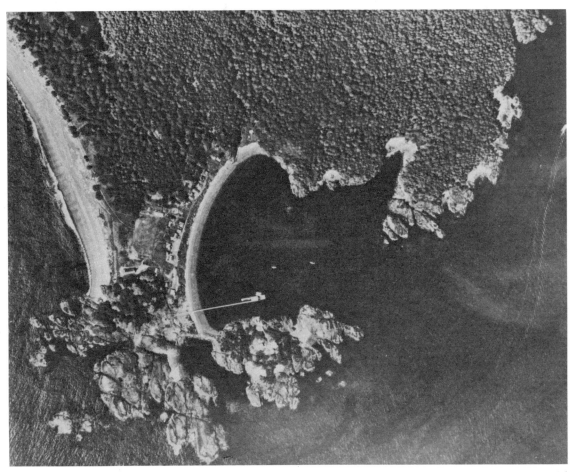

24

24 British Columbia Aerial Survey photo, courtesy
Dr. John Steelquist.

Nootka: Aerial photograph of Friendly Cove
taken in 1972 from an altitude of 4,000 feet.
Note the striking similarity to the 1791 plan on
the opposite page. Considering that the cartog-
raphers of the Malaspina Expedition were
unable to have the bird's-eye-view afforded by
aerial photography, their creation is all the more
remarkable for its accuracy.

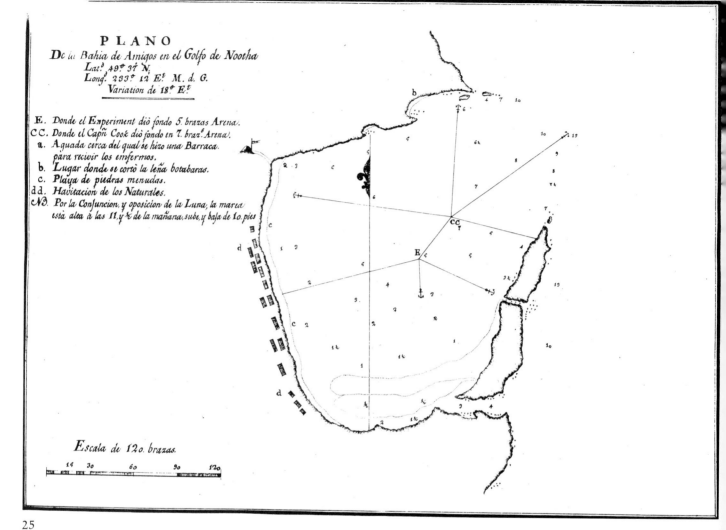

PLANO
De la Bahia de Amigos en el Golfo de Nootha
Lat.ᵈ 49.° 37' N,
Long.ᵈ 233.° 12' E.ᵗ M. d. G.
Variation de 18.ᵗ E.ᵗ

E. Donde el Experiment diò fondo 5. brazas Arena.
CC. Donde el Capñ Cook diò fondo en 7. braz.ˢ Arena.
a. Aguada cerca del qual se hizo una Barraca.
    para recivir los enfermos.
b. Lugar donde se cortò la leña botabaras.
c. Playa de piedras menudas.
dd. Havitacion de los Naturales.
NB. Por la Confuncion, y oposicion de la Luna; la marea
    està alta à las 11,y ½ de la mañana, sube, y baja de 10. pies

Escala de 120. brazas.

15   30   60   90   120

25

25 Archivo General de Indias Coll.

Nootka: The "pozo" (a) here refers to a well
with good water which is adjacent to the hospital or infirmary; (b) notes where firewood is cut;
(c) identifies the beach of small stones; (CC) is
the Cook anchorage with the new letters introduced by Vicente Tofino in the 1770s; (A) is
sand and gravel; and (E) anchored in 5 fathoms
could mean the *Descubierta* (Discovery), although the notes says *Experiment*.

Plano.
Del Puerto de Yucuat
Situado en la Parte Occidental
de la Entrada de Nutka. Trava
jado Abordo de las Corvetas Mar.
Marina P.l Descur.ta y Atrev.
Año de 1791.

Lat.d N. . . . 49° 35' 15"
Long.d Oc.l de C. 120° 33' 42"

26 Museo Naval Coll.

Nootka: "Plan of the port of Yacuat situated in the eastern part of the entrance to Nootka drawn at the time of the *Descubierta* and *Atrevida* in 1791" might refer to the Yuquot or the lookout station used by the Indian whale hunters on Hog Island. "Pozo" in this case means a well.

27

27 [Jose Cardero?], *A view of Puerto de Nunez
Gaona* [sic Nootka]. Inscription: "Vista del
Puerto de Nunez Gaona." Museo de America
Coll. (Bauza No. 12). Watercolor. 24.8 x 42.4
cm.

This is a perplexing problem, perhaps undis-
cussed hitherto. The drawing is attributed to
Cardero but since we believe it to be misidentified it may very well be the work of another.
The commanding fort in the upper left must
surely be San Miguel in Puerto de Santa Cruz at
Nootka, surmounted by the flag of Spain. John
Boit on the *Columbia* described the fort as "no
great thing," but it was there. In the middle
ground rides a corvette which is probably the

Princesa, which is frequently misidentified and
over-gunned—we think she carried 36. A further problem is the war canoe with the distinc-
tive carved eagle, which we do associate with
Puerto de Nunez Gaona's much more open bay,
thought generally unsatisfactory for this reason
plus its poor bottom. But all the background
detail is assuredly Nootka. The harbor is Santa
Cruz or Friendly Harbor, and includes the observatory tents, the dwellings, gardens and even

the very clear beach (beaches usually were clear before the advent of heavy logging which stimulated the buildup of driftwood and logs along all of the Pacific shoreline).

Essentially this work is not in Cardero's style and it might be that this drawing was "prepared" by an assistant in Mexico City or Madrid, or perhaps Cardero himself did the work for the eventual drawing which faithfully follows this enriched version.

28 Fernando Brambila, *View of the settlement and port of Nootka.* Inscription: "Vista de establecimiento y puerto de Nutka." Museo Naval Coll. 47 x 25 cm.

This interesting view must be taken with a grain of salt because it appears to be one of the drawings "improved" by Brambila. The topography has been changed somewhat but still conveys the feeling of Santa Cruz de Nuca as it appeared at the time of the "Controversy" and Malaspina's visit. The "pozo" or spring located on some of the charts drawn by Malaspina's staff would be approximately over the flagstaff of the trading vessel on the right. And at least for this painting the natives have returned in force.

Establecimiento de Nutka 2°

29

29 [Jose Cardero], *Nootka*. Inscription: "Establecimiento de Nutka 2°." Museo de America Coll. (Bauza No. 21). Watercolor sketch. 21.6 x 42.2 cm.

Similar to Bauza No. 12. Donald Cutter attributes this important sketch to Cardero. While not the finished drawing which precedes this entry, the canvas observatory is clearly shown with flap up perhaps for the busy scientists and recorders. A William Bayly tent design is seen, as in the magnificent Webber drawings of Cook's anchorage at Nootka. No sign of life is seen on the beach where the tide is in, but a barely discernible penciled gig moves shoreward. One might suppose the major construction underway might be the Commandant's house or the barracks for this distant colonial outpost, which were built mainly by Chinese laborers and Spanish soldiers and sailors.

30 [Felipe Bauza?], *View of the first Spanish settlement at Nootka.* Inscription: "Establecimiento de Nutka, 1°." Museo de America Coll. (Bauza No. 20). Watercolor. 22.2 x 41.4 cm.

The simple drawing shows several huts in front of a luxuriant forest; there is a cross in the center installed by the Spanish friars. On the right a larger dwelling could possibly be the one occupied by Captain John Meares. The port of Nootka, on the shores of which this settlement was located, was called Friendly Cove by Cook. Esteban Martinez called it Santa Cruz. Inside the fences are what we believe to be the first vegetable gardens in the Pacific Northwest, which were planted the preceding year. We do not know to whom to attribute this sketch, but because the style is similar to another known to be by Bauza, we are inclined to think of him. The early Malaspina sketches show no natives on the beach or on the water, since all were hiding in the deep forest.

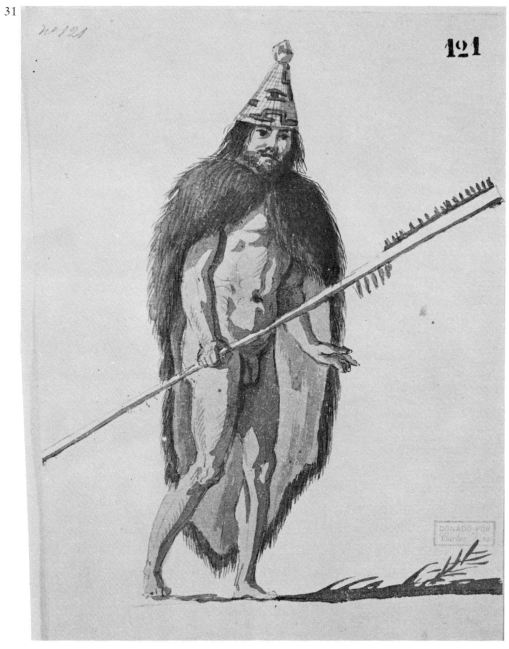

31 [Tomas de Suria or Felipe Bauza], *An Indian of Nootka.* Inscription: "Yndio de Nutka." Museo de America Coll. (Bauza No. 121). Ink and wash. 19.9 x 14.9 cm.

We see a native of Nootka wearing a classic hat of woven fernstem and grasses or spruce roots. The heavy cloak, which may be a bearskin, covers his shoulders; the rest of the body is nude and apparently hairless below the chin. In his right hand he holds a herring rake about 20 feet long. His covering reveals that he is a chief. We hesitate to attribute this drawing to de Suria, although the account of the voyage remarks that the painter from Mexico did a portrait of Macuina which "has especially captured the spirit of this chief, as have all the others which he did at Nootka." A jaunty drawing from the Cook stay at Nootka fifteen years earlier is faithful in detail, even to the design and height (90 cm.) of the conical hat.

32 [Tomas de Suria], *A woman of Nootka.* Inscription: "Muger de Nutka." Museo de America Coll. (Bauza No. 45). Ink and wash. 16.5 x 65 cm.

A young woman wearing around her shoulders a typical cape made of cypress bark interwoven with fur and goat hair. Matzapi's second wife?

33

34

33 [Jose Cardero], *Portrait of the second wife of Tetaku.* Inscription: "Segunda Muger de Tetaku." Museo de America Coll. (Bauza No. 60). Watercolor. 26.1 x 23 cm.

The features of this woman are very similar to those of the adjacent drawing. We believe that this drawing was also prepared for engraving by Selma. In addition to the personality of the woman which is evident, the portrait is of interest for the detail of her adornments. A report on the finery worn by the women at the entrance to Fuca reads: "They wear many bracelets, either of copper or of raven scalps, collars of shells, copper or of glass beads. In the same mode they adorn the ears and nose with hanging pendants, the ears and nose always being pierced, and they use red and black pigments on themselves; they use grease to make their hair shine, and they are much more careful in their extravagant adornments than are the Nootka Indians."

34 [Jose Cardero ?], *Portrait of Maria, wife of Tetaku, with a child in her arms.* Inscription: "Muger de Tetaku, de la Entrada de Fuca." Museo de America Coll. (Bauza No. 59). Watercolor. 26.2 x 20.2 cm.

This too is believed to be a portrait of Maria, favorite wife of Tetaku. The drawing is done in minute detail and shows a young woman with artistically Asiatic features, adorned with a headdress, nose ornament, long pendant ear ornaments and necklace; she is wearing a finely woven fibre cape nicely ornamented with fur; in her arms she holds an infant wrapped in a similar woven covering, and wearing a conical head covering, perhaps for skull shaping. It is possible that the previous drawing of Maria may have served as the model, with certain changes, for this more finished realization, although her ear pendants and wrapper appear to be the same.

35

36

35 Jose Cardero, *Portrait of one of the wives of Tetaku*. Inscription: "Muger de Tetaku A'ancau de Fuca." Museo de America Coll. (Bauza No. 58). Watercolor. 26 x 20.5 cm.

Cardero probably made this drawing during the survey made by the schooners *Sutil* and *Mexicana*. The woman is Maria, the favorite wife of Tetaku. On June 8, 1792, the schooners were in the Puerto de Nunez Gaona (Neah Bay) at the entrance to the Strait of Juan de Fuca; there Tetaku declared friendship with the officers and introduced them to his wife. The clothing, dentalium, brass bead ornaments and the woman's features are clearly shown with the fidelity which marks Cardero's work.

36 [Jose Cardero], *Portrait of Tetaku*. Inscription: "Gefe de la entrada de Juan de Fuca, Tetaku." Museo de America Coll. (Bauza No. 57). Watercolor. 26.2 x 20.4 cm.

This drawing shows the Chief (Tetakus, Tetacu, Tatooch) whose description and friendship toward the officers of the schooners are noted in the *Relacion*: "Tetakus [*sic*] is one of the principal chiefs of the entrance (to Fuca), and according to confirmed reports, he was one of the most friendly to the Spaniards." His friendship was such that he introduced his favorite wife to the Spaniards, and decided to go with them as they explored the inner channels. A drawing very similar to this is to be found in the Museo Naval in Madrid, and his hat resembles that worn by "A Man of Nootka" painted by John Webber in April, 1778.

37

37 [Jose Cardero], *Indian fortification at the entrance to the Strait of Juan de Fuca.* Inscription: "Forificacion de los Yndios del estrecho de Fuca." Museo de America Coll.

(Bauza No. 7). Watercolor. 28.5 x 42.5 cm. Although this drawing bears the inscription "Indian fortification," it appears more likely that it was constructed by the Spanish. It could be the Spanish "establecimiento" which Salvador Fidalgo built at Nuñez Gaona on the south shore of the Strait of Juan de Fuca, in expectation of orders he was to receive from Commander Bodega y Quadra. In Chapter V of the *Relacion* one finds the following description which relates to the drawing: "Fidalgo has arrived and had land dug up to make a garden and he has already had trees planted in it. . .there is a large corral for livestock, for the cattle, sheep, pigs and goats. Near this there is a barracks where they keep a guard to attend to the custody and maintain everything in order, hastening the work so that they will be ready to winter if need arises. . . . The land appears more fruitful than at Nootka, and the climate milder and more salubrious, watered by small rivers and protected by forests and high mountains." However all of this livestock and activity was transferred in 1792 to Nootka by order of Revillagigedo, Viceroy in Mexico City.

50 / VOYAGES OF ENLIGHTENMENT

38 Jose Cardero, *View of the settlement of Maguaa.* Inscription: "Vista de la Gran Rancheria de Maguaa." Museo de America Coll. (Bauza No. 37). Watercolor. 27.4 x 43.3 cm.

In the foregound four men are paddling a chief wrapped in furs; in the middle ground are two schooners, undoubtedly the *Sutil* and *Mexicana*, surrounded by trading canoes; in the background is a substantial settlement ringed by a dense forest. Three mountains dominate the horizon. The dwellings run in a typical straggle along the beach. The drawing signed by Cardero was probably intended to be finished for the engraver by Cardero himself, either in Madrid under the guidance of Brambila, or perhaps during the voyage. If the schooners are the *Sutil* and the *Mexicana*, the drawing must have been done during the 1792 phase of the exploration. One wonders whether "Maguaa" may not be Majoa," a settlement in the labyrinthine channels which the schooners visited on the northwest part of Vancouver Island. The two ships were the first to circumnavigate this 285-mile long island followed soon after by Captain George Vancouver.

39 *The* Sutil *and* Mexicana. Museo Naval Coll.
The *Sutil* and *Mexicana* trailing their boats with
Mount Baker [?] in background.

These 46-ton schooners laid down in San Blas
naval yards no doubt provided a rude surprise
to Captain George Vancouver when he first
encountered them deep in the Strait of Georgia,
late in June, 1792. Until then the English sur-
veyor supposed that he was first through the
Strait with his *Discovery* and *Chatham*. Unfortunately Vancouver's original journal has
never been found, but in time we may learn his
real feelings upon this friendly encounter. A sea
otter or seal spear projects from the beautifully
shaped canoe.

52 / *VOYAGES OF ENLIGHTENMENT*

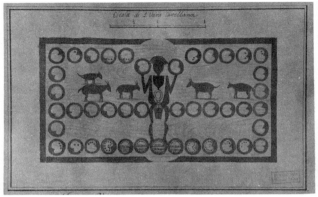

41

40

42

40 [Jose Cardero], *Portrait of a Chief of Puerto del Descanso.* Inscription: "Gefe del Puerto del Descanso." Museo de America Coll. (Bauza No. 55). Watercolor. 26.3 x 20.7 cm.

The schooners were exploring from the 12th to the 15th of August. In the Puerto del Descanso and its environs they observed that most were squint-eyed. This area and its inhabitants are described at length in the *Relacion* of the voyage. We surmise that the drawing was made by Cardero of a chief from Nanaimo.

41 [Jose Cardero], *Copy of hieroglyphic designs drawn on a plank of wood found by Valdes on a hill on the east coast of the Strait of Juan de Fuca.* Inscription: "Tabla de 2 1/2. varas de largo, encontrada en el Canal de su nombre." Museo de America Coll. (Bauza No. 42). Ink.

17.2 x 25.5 cm.
In the *Relacion del viaje de las goletas*. . .we find a note: "At nightfall Valdes returned with the cutter, having explored a sizeable arm which he called La Tabla [The Plank], because on the east coast of it he had seen on a hill a kind of wooden plank on which were represented various hieroglyphics." This drawing of a highly

stylized human accompanied by five goats was engraved and reproduced in the *Atlas del viage de las Goletas* as No. 16. It is attributed to Cardero because he was the artist who accompanied this expedition; while it could have been done by another officer, this appears unlikely.

42 [Jose Cardero], *Portrait of an Indian from Salida de las Goletas (Island of Quadra and Vancouver).* Inscription: "Yndio de la Costa NO. en la salida de las Goletas." Museo de America Coll. (Bauza No. 56). Watercolor. 26.2 x 20.6 cm.

The Kwakiutl portrait, probably by Cardero, shows a native from Puerto de Guemes near Queen Charlotte Strait, through which the schooners were threading. The man wears a headpiece of ermine or feathers with pendant side pieces. He has painted his face with a kind of ochre mixed with oil. Men and women daubed their faces with red, white and black paint "with various scrawls." His ears are hung with shell pendants, perhaps of "Monterrey shell." It is likely that a sea otter pelt covers his shoulders, similar to those used at the entrance to the Strait of Juan de Fuca. He wears an arm-bracelet, probably of copper, and pectoral markings.

43 [Jose Cardero or Fernando Brambila], *View of Salamanca Channel.* Inscription: "Vista del Remate del Canal de Salamanca y sospechoso seguimiento de los Yndios." Museo de America Coll. (Bauza No. 6). Ink. 31.5 x 54 cm.

Salamanca Channel was named after an officer, Secondino Salamanca, who explored this area as part of the second-phase exploration around Vancouver Island by *Sutil* and *Mexicana*. A similar drawing, although inferior in quality, exists in the Museo Naval, and is attributed to Cardero; it may have been used as a sketch for this one by either Cardero himself or by Brambila. The water is alive with importuning natives and explorers appear on the *qui vive*. A two-hatch baidarka (right) and somber trees add interest to the scene.

44 Jose Cardero, *View of Puerto de Nunez Gaona.*
Inscription: "Vista del Establecimiento Espanol
en el Puerto de Nunez Gaona y gran Canoa de
Guerra de Tetaku." Museo de America Coll.
(Bauza No. 13). Ink. 27.5 x 43 cm.

In the foreground is observed a war canoe filled

with natives; one man is standing, probably
Tetaku, a nearby chief. In the background a corvette is seen, probably the *Princesa* under the
command of Salvador Fidalgo, and behind her,
the schooners *Sutil* and *Mexicana.* The *Relacion*
gives the following observation concerning
Tetaku's canoe: ". . .the canoe has a great carved
eaglet on the prow, a figure which we have
often seen on other war canoes. The Indians
seem to attach a certain feeling of fear or of
veneration to the effigy of this bird, as do the
California natives who are particularly grateful
to it for having rescued (they say) an Indian
from a whirlpool." Curiously, Tetaku appears
with the same crew and rowers in the finished
view of Friendly Cove far to the north (Bauza
No. 12)—such a striking ensemble attracted artistic license in faraway studios.

45 [Jose Cardero], *View of Bernac[c]i Channel inside the entrance to the Strait of Juan de Fuca.* Inscription: "Vista del Canal de Bernaci y una gran Cascada." Museo de America Coll. (Bauza No. 4). Watercolor. 31.6 x 53.9 cm.

The drawing shows the armed cutter used for exploring from the schooners *Sutil* and *Mexicana.* On the right are seen high rocks from which a large cascade of water falls, and several Indian canoes issuing from a cove in the inlet. In the background is a snow-covered mountain range [the Olympics?]. A description of this place is to be found in the *Relacion:* "We have encountered places with lovely views, rather high lands covered with trees, and meadows and many fine deep beaches. . . . In one we had to admire a waterfall of melted snow. . .cascad-

ing into/the channel with great noise, causing a disturbance in the air." This drawing is attributed to Cardero, since if it was not finished by him it was made after a sketch of his which is preserved in the Museo Naval in Madrid. The man standing up in the stern sheets seems to be sketching the scene, which only an artist would do.

46 Fernando Brambila, *View of Acapulco*.
Inscription: "Vista de la Poblacion y Puerto de
ACAPULCO Sacada desde el fronton del
Grito." Museo de America Coll. (Bauza No. 23).
23 x 16 cm.

The beautiful harbor of Acapulco shows to
best advantage in this finished drawing by
Fernando Brambila. Brambila arrived from Italy
to join the explorers aboard the *Atrevida* upon
the Expedition's return from the Northwest
Coast. Brambila was a skilled artist whose Italian
patrons had sent him to Malaspina. He improved a number of Cardero's accurate but less
polished depictions of northern life.

A generation of colonial officials favored this
port over fever-ridden San Blas, but a constant
supply of fresh water and hardwood gave the
advantage to the more northerly located San
Blas. The Expedition left this harbor for the
Marianas and surveys of the Philippine Islands.
In the 19th century both ports subsided and
languished in inactivity.

MALASPINA ON THE NORTHWEST COAST / 57

Selected Bibliography

Aria Divito, Juan Carlos. *Las expediciones cientificas espanolas durante el siglo XVIII.* Madrid, 1968.

Barras de Aragon, Francisco de las. "Los Rusos en el Noroeste de America." *Anales de la Asociacion Espanola para el progreso de las ciencias*, 31. Madrid, 1956: 111-26.

Barreiro-Meiro, Roberto, editor. *Coleccion de diarios y relaciones para la historia de los viajes descubrimientos*, 7. Madrid, 1975.

Barry, John Neilson. "Broughton on the Columbia in 1792." *Oregon Historical Quarterly*, 27 (1926): 397-411.
"Broughton, Up the Columbia River, 1792." *OHQ* 32 (1931): 301-12.
"Columbia River Exploration, 1792." *OHQ* 33 (1932): 31-42, 143-55.
"Who Discovered the Columbia River?" *OHQ* 39 (1938): 152-61.

Beaglehole, John C. *The Journals of Captain James Cook on His Voyages of Discovery*, Vol. 3 *The Voyage of the* Resolution *and* Discovery. Cambridge, 1967.
The Life of Captain James Cook. Stanford, Calif., 1974.

Berkh, Vasilii Nikolaevich. *Khronologicheskaia istoriia otkrytiia aleutskiks ostrovov.* St. Petersburg, 1823. English edition, *The Chronological History of the Discovery of the Aleutian Islands or the Exploits of the Russian Merchants.* Seattle, 1938.

Bodega y Quadra, Juan Francisco de la. "Navegacion hecha por Don Juan Francisco de la Bodega y Quadra, Teniente de Fragata de la Real Armada y comandante de la goleta 'Sonora': A los descubrimientos de los mares y costa septentrional de California." *Coleccion de diarios y relaciones para la historia de los viajes y descubrimientos*, 2. Madrid, 1943: 102-33.

Boone, Lalla Rookh. "Vancouver on the Northwest Coast." *OHQ* 35 (1934): 193-227.

Brand, Donald Dilworth. "The Development of Pacific Coast Ports During the Spanish Colonial Period in Mexico." *Estudios antropologicos publicados en homenaje al Doctor Manuel Gamio.* Mexico City, 1956: 577-91.

[Cardero, Jose]. *Relacion del viaje hecho por las goletas "Sutil" y "Mexicana" en el ano de 1792.* 1 volume and atlas. Madrid, 1802.

Carey, Charles H. "Some Early Maps and Myths." *OHQ* 30 (1929): 14-32.

Carril, Bonifacio del. *La expedicion Malaspina en los mares americanos del sur: la coleccion Bauza, 1789-1794.* Buenos Aires, 1961.

Caselli, Carlo. *Alessandro Malaspina e la sua*

spedizione scientifica intorno al mondo, con documenti inediti. Milan, 1929.

Castillo Ledon, Luis. "El Puerto de San Blas. Su fundacion y su historia." *Boletin de la Sociedad Mexicana de Geografia y Estadistica*, 60. 1945: 583-95.

Chapman, Charles Edward. "The Difficulties of Maintaining the Department of San Blas, 1775-1777." *Southwestern Historical Quarterly*, 19 (1915-16): 261-70.
The Founding of Spanish California: the Northwestward Expansion of New Spain, 1687-1773. New York, 1916.
A History of California: the Spanish Period. New York, 1921.

Convencion entre el Rey nuestro senor y el Rey de la Gran Bretana, transigiendo varios puntos sobre pesca, navegacion y comercio en el Oceano Pacifico y los mares del sur, firmada en San Lorenzo el Real a 28 de octubre de 1790, cuyas ratificaciones se canjearon en el mismo sitio a 22 de noviembre siguiente. Madrid, [1790?].

Cook, James. *A Voyage to the Pacific Ocean.* 3 volumes and atlas. London, 1784.

Cook, Warren L. *Flood Tide of Empire: Spain and the Pacific Northwest, 1543-1819.* New Haven, 1973.

Cutter, Donald C. *Malaspina in California.* San Francisco, 1960.
"Spanish Scientific Exploration along the Pacific Coast." *The American West: an Appraisal.* Robert G. Ferris, ed. Santa Fe, 1963.
"Spain and the Oregon Coast." *The Western Shore: Oregon Country Essays honoring the American Revolution.* Thomas Vaughan, ed. Portland, 1975: 29-46.

Elliott, Thompson Coit. "Cook's Journal of His Approach to Oregon." *OHQ* 29 (1928): 265-77. "The Oregon Coast as Seen by Vancouver in 1792." *OHQ* 30 (1929): 33-42, 384-394.

Engstrand, Iris H. Wilson. "Scientists in New Spain: The Eighteenth Century Expeditions." *The Spanish Borderlands: A First Reader.* Oakah Jones, ed. Los Angeles, 1974.

Estrada, Rafael. *El viaje de las corbetas "Descubierta" y "Atrevida" y los artistas de la expedicion, 1789-1794.* Madrid, 1930.

Fernandez Duro, Cesareo. *La Armada Espanola desde la union de los reinos de Castilla y de Aragon.* 9 volumes. Madrid, 1895-1903. "Tadeo Haenke, naturalista en el viaje alrededor del mundo de las corbetas 'Descubierta' y 'Atrevida', al mando de Alejandro Malaspina, desde 1789 a 1794." *Boletin academia de la historia,* 39 (1901).

Fernandez, Justino. *Tomas de Suria y su viaje con Malaspina.* Mexico City, 1939.

Ferrari Bono, Bruno P. *El viage de Malaspina y su vinculacion en el movimiento revolucionario.* Buenos Aires, 1960.

Ferrer Maldonado, Lorenzo. "Relacion del descubrimiento del Estrecho de Anian que hice yo...en el ano de 1588..." In Alejandro Malaspina, *Viaje politico-cientifico. . . .* Madrid, 1885: 137-44.

Galbraith, Edith C. "Malaspina's Voyage around the World." *California Historical Society Quarterly,* 3 (1924): 215-37.

Ganiushkina, T., R. Razumovskaya, and I. Shavrina. *Museum of Anthropology and Ethnography.* Leningrad, 1973.

Gibson, James R. "Bostonians and Muscovites on the Northwest Coast, 1788-1841." *The Western Shore: Oregon Country Essays honoring the American Revolution.* Thomas Vaughan, ed. Portland, 1975: 81-120.

Gough, Barry M. "The Northwest Coast in Late 18th Century British Expansion." *The Western Shore.* Portland, 1975: 47-80.

Grepi, E. "Un italiano alla corte de Spagna nel Secolo XVIII. Alezandro Malaspina." *Nuova Antologia.* Marzo, 1883.

Gunther, Erna. *Indian Life on the Northwest Coast of North America.* Chicago, 1972.

Hernandez y Sanchez-Barba, Mario. "Espanoles, Rusos e Ingleses en el Pacifico Norte, durante el siglo XVIII." *Informacion juridica*, 121. Madrid, 1953: 549-66.

Howay, Frederick William. "Early Navigation of the Straits of Fuca." *OHQ* 12 (1911): 1-32. "The Spanish Settlement at Nootka." *Washington Historical Quarterly*, 8 (1917): 163-71.

Humboldt, Alexander von. *Essai politique sur le royaume de la Nouvelle Espagne.* 4 volumes and atlas. Paris, 1811.

Humphreys, Robin A. "Richard Oswald's Plan for an English and Russian Attack on Spanish America, 1781-1782." *Hispanic American Historical Review*, 18 (1938): 95-101.

Krasheninnikov, Stepan Petrovich. *Opizanie Zemli Kamchatki.* St. Petersburg, 1755. English edition, *Explorations of Kamchatka: North Pacific Scimitar.* E.A.P. Crownhart-Vaughan, translator and editor. Portland, 1972.

Macintyre, Captain Donald, R.N. *Admiral Rod-ney.* New York, 1962.

Malaspina, Alejandro. *Viage al Rio de la Plata en el siglo XVIII.* Buenos Aires, 1938. *Viaje politico-cientifico alrededor del mundo por las corbetas "Descubierta" y "Atrevida."* Introduction by Pedro Novo y Colson. Madrid, 1885.

Martinez, Esteban Jose. *Coleccion de diarios y relaciones para la historia de los viajes y descubrimientos*, 6. Madrid, 1964. "Diario de la Navegacion que Yo el Alf(ere)z. de Navio de la R(ea)l. Arm(a)da. D(o). Estevan Josef Martinez boy a executar al P(uer)to. de S(a)n. Carlos. . .1789." Edited by Roberto Barreiro-Meiro. *Coleccion de diarios y relaciones para la historia de los viajes y descubrimientos.* 6. Madrid, 1964: 19-148.

Morse, William I., editor. *Letters of Alejandro Malaspina (1790-1791).* Boston, 1944.

Mozino Suarez de Figueroa, Jose Mariano. *Noticias de Nutka. Diccionario de la lengua de los Nutkeses y descripcion del volcan de Tuxtla.* Mexico City, 1913. English edition, *Noticias de Nutka, an Account of Nootka Sound in 1792.* Iris Higbie Wilson, translator and editor. Seattle, 1970.

Navarro Garcia, Luis de. "El norte de Nueva Espana como problema politico en el siglo XVIII." *Revista estudios americanos*, 103 Seville, 1960: 15-31.

Novo y Colson, Pedro. *Historia de las exploraciones articas hechas en busca del paso del nordeste.* Madrid, 1880.

Official papers relative to the dispute between the courts of Great Britain and Spain on the subject of the ships captured in Nootka

Sound, and the negotiation that followed thereon. London, 1790.

Palau, Mercedes. *Chile en las Expediciones Cientificas Espanolas de siglos XVII y XIX.* Madrid, 1976.

Priestly, Herbert Ingram. "The Log of the Princesa by Estevan Martinez: What does It Contribute to Our Knowledge of the Nootka Sound Controversy?" *OHQ* 21 (1920): 21-31.

Ramos Catalina y de Bardazi, Maria Luisa. "Expediciones cientificas a California el en siglo XVIII." *Anuario de estudios americanos*, 217-230.

Rasmussen, Louise. "Artists with Explorations on the Northwest Coast." *OHQ* 42 (1941): 311-16.

"Short Account of Some Voyages Made by Order of the King of Spain, to Discover the State of the West American Coast from California Upward. Dated Madrid, 24 March, 1776." *Summary observations and facts collected from late and authentic accounts of Russian and other navigators, to show the practicability and good prospect of success in enterprises to discover a northern passage for vessels by sea, between the Atlantic and Pacific Oceans.* London, 1776.

Taylor, George P. "Spanish-Russian Rivalry in the Pacific, 1769-1820." *The Americas*, 25 (1958): 109-27.

Thurman, Michael E. "The Establishment of the Department of San Blas and Its Initial Naval Fleet: 1767-1770." *HAHR* 43 (1963): 65-67. *The Naval Department of San Blas, New Spain's Bastion for Alta California and Nootka, 1767 to 1798.* Glendale, California, 1967.

Torre Revello, Jose. *Los artistas pintores de la expedicion Malaspina.* Buenos Aires, 1944.

Vancouver, George. *A voyage of discovery to the North Pacific Ocean and round the world.* 3 volumes and atlas. London, 1789.

Vela, V. Vicente. "Expedicion de Malaspina: Epistolario referente a su organizacion." *Revista de Indias*, 11 (1951): 193-218.

Wagner, Henry Raup. "The Last Spanish Exploration of the Northwest Coast and the Attempt to Colonize Bodega Bay." *CHSQ* 9 (1931): 313-45.
Spanish Explorations in the Strait of Juan de Fuca. Santa Ana, California, 1933.
"Journal of Tomas de Suria of His Voyage with Malaspina to the Northwest Coast of America in 1791." *PHR* 5 (1936): 234-39.
The Cartography of the Northwest Coast of America to the Year 1800. Berkeley, 1937.

Young, Frederick George. "Spain and England's Quarrel over the Oregon Country." *OHQ* 21 (1920): 13-20.